With my deepest personal regards

Harry Lauder

The Last of
the Numbered Men

THE LAST OF THE
NUMBERED MEN

A Memoir of the Holocaust

Harry Posmantier

All proceeds from sales of *The Last of the Numbered Men* will be donated to the following nonprofit organizations: The Washington Memorial of the Holocaust, The Women's American O.R.T., Mogen David Adom (Red Cross), and Yad Vashem in Jerusalem.

FIRST EDITION

All rights reserved, including the right of reproduction in whole or in part in any form.

Copyright © 1984 by Harry Posmantier

Published by Vantage Press, Inc.
516 West 34th Street, New York, New York 10001

Manufactured in the United States of America
ISBN: 533-05956-9

Library of Congress Catalog Card No.: 83-90957

To the memory of all those who perished in the Holocaust,
and to my parents, who taught me to love life

Out of the ashes of the Holocaust, the nation of Israel was born, and out of that suffering my soul became crystallized. I gained understanding—of freedom, of human dignity, and of life itself. As I finished recording the last chapter of my war years, I discharged a burden that I had carried in the back of my mind since the day I was liberated by the American Third Army.

Now I am at peace. I have written the last sentences of my past, but there are more than six million other stories that will never be told.

I have written my story with great agony and great love, in the hope that my children and grandchildren, who sleep safely in their own beds at night, will never awaken from a nightmare to find it has become reality. May God bless and protect them and their descendants. Amen.

Contents

A Legacy		xi
Introduction		xiii
Prologue: Separation		xvii
Part I:	Growing Up	1
	Bendin	3
	To Palestine	12
	War Clouds	17
	War	22
	Homeward Bound	27
	Bendsburg	34
	The People's Court	37
Part II:	The Camps	47
	R.A.B. Lager Klein Mangersdorf	49
	R.A.B. Lager Rogau	62
	Z.A.L. Annaberg	65
	Z.A.L. Ottmuth	68
	Z.A.L. Blechhammer	76
	Z.A.L. Brande	84
	Z.A.L. Sagan	87
	K.Z. Blechhammer/Auschwitz III	102
	The Bloody March	120
	K.Z. Gross Rossen	123
	K.Z. Bissingen	140
	K.Z. Allach Dachau	144
	Staltach Junction	150
	Artilerie Kaserne Landsberg Lech	158
	Epilogue	179

A Legacy

To my children and their children and their children's children, I hereby give a legacy: On April 30, each and every year, the anniversary of my liberation by the American army and of Adolph Hitler's death, the story of the plight of the Jewish people during World War II shall be retold so they shall never forget what the Germans under Nazi rule did to them. Prayers and donations shall be made in memory of those of our family who perished, so their memories shall be carried on, forever and ever. Their trials shall be remembered to guard against the chance that at any future time human beings will again be numbered and slaughtered like cattle, and to insure that my generation contains the last of the numbered men.

—H.P.

Mom and Dad in 1938

Introduction

October, 1982. The Holocaust. Six million Jews and many millions of non-Jews from all over Europe were put to death.

Many, however, survived, each with a story of his own to tell. Each survivor encountered at least one miracle.

The world lost much in dignity, innocence, and talent. It is impossible to know how many Einsteins, Salks, Tellers, and Oppenheimers were destroyed. How different the world might have been! The loss to all humanity will reverberate for many generations to come.

The Jewish contribution to the world in such fields as science, medicine, commerce, art, politics, physics, law, and journalism has been immeasurable. There have been more Jewish Nobel–prize winners than from any nation on Earth. How much more greatness would there have been?

The Jewish suffering under Hitler was beyond comprehension. Had I not been a witness to those atrocities, I would never have believed that this could have happened in a civilized nation in the twentieth century. My only hope is that such cruelty of man to man can be avoided in the future.

It has been agonizing for me to bring all this to paper, to relive the horrors of the war and its aftermath. My writing was prompted by my grandson, Eric, who one day several years ago asked me, "Grandpa, why do you have a number on your arm?"

How could I explain to a lovable little three-year-old child what that number—178246—represents? I told him I was in something like a military camp, where we were numbered, and promised that, when he grew older, I would tell him the story of the numbered people. It was then that I decided to put my story into writing, and so this book was born.

It is a recollection of my war years. It is intended to give a feel for the horror and the grim humor of those years, not to provide accurate dates or statistics. It is already thirty-seven years after the war, and the events I recollect may not concur with the detail of some history texts. To those who find details in error, my apologies in advance.

What I remember is the camps I lived through from 1940 until the Third Army liberated me and those who remained of my fellow prisoners at the railroad junction in Staltach, Bavaria, on April 30, 1945. To my liberators, my eternal gratitude.

The camps I passed through, in order of incarceration, were:

1.	R.A.B.* Klein Mangersdorf III	1940
2.	R.A.B. Rogau	1941
3.	Z.A.L.** Annaberg	1941
4.	Z.A.L. Ottmuth	1941–42
5.	Z.A.L. Blechhammer	1942
6.	Z.A.L. Brande	1942
7.	Z.A.L. Sagan	1942–43
8.	K.Z.† Blechhammer/Auschwitz III	1943–45
9.	K.Z. Gross Rosen	1945
10.	K.Z. Buchenwald	1945
11.	K.Z. Bissingen	1945
12.	K.Z. Allach-Dachau	1945

To my family, I give special thanks for encouraging me to write of my experiences. While the writing was agony, through it I have found a measure of peace.

*R.A.B.: *Reichsautobahnlager* (German Highway Camp).
**Z.A.L.: *Zwangarbeitslager* (Forced Labor Camp).
†K.Z.: *Kazetlager* (Concentration Camp).

This book is for my dear wife, Ruth; my son, David, and his wife, Lynn; my daughter, Beth, who corrected my spelling; my grandson, Eric; my granddaughter, Sarranna Nicole, and all my dear friends, with all my love.

I also offer my deep gratitude to my friend Richard Greb, who edited my writings, and his wife, Sue, who typed my text from longhand. Without them, this book could never have been printed.

Prologue: Separation

Bendsburg
October 20, 1940

Dear Sir:

You are hereby requested to appear before a medical board of examiners on October 27th, at 8:00 o'clock A.M. in the Orphanage for Jewish Children, by order of the German Government and the Gauleiter for East Oberschlesien. You are to bring with you clothes for three months and food for one day.

The Jewish Board of Elders for the Town of Bendsburg o/s*

Sunday, October 27, 1940, was a cloudy, drizzly day. The clouds hung low, dark, and heavy and looked likely at any minute to burst into thousands upon thousands of tears. At 6:00 A.M., I said goodbye to my two younger brothers. I took the plywood suitcase into which I had packed my belongings the night before and, accompanied by my father and mother, walked the two kilometers to the orphanage. Two Jewish policemen at the gate checked my notice and let me in. My parents had to remain outside.

Inside were 250 youths between eighteen and twenty-eight

---

*This translation may not correspond exactly to the original notification.

years old, all of whom I knew from school and work but many I hadn't seen in years. We exchanged greetings as we waited for the unknown. There was only one thing we knew for sure: we were to be shipped into slave labor in Germany.

At exactly 8:00 A.M., five doctors, accompanied by Jewish policemen, appeared. We were ordered to undress, form a line, and, in Adam's clothes, proceed to the rooms into which the examining doctors had gone. We were called in alphabetical order and each given a number. I became 118, losing at that moment my identity and becoming for the duration only digits.

The doctors' procedures were routine. In the first room I was asked a few questions about previous illnesses, and my heartbeat was checked with a stethoscope. In the second room, my vision was examined, and in the third my mouth and throat. In the fourth room, the remaining doctors marked my medical record *"faehig"* (able).

I was told to dress, take my things, and join the rest of the "able" in the dining room.

At 11:00 A.M., the examinations were complete, and we were mustered outside and counted. Two hundred of us had passed the physical examination.

At exactly 11:30, a truck pulled up in front of the orphanage and sixteen brownshirts got out. These men, whose nickname came from the color of their uniforms, were stormtroopers, Sturmapteilung (S.A.), members of the military branch of the Nazi party. The S.A. had been formed in 1923 and was eventually incorporated into the S.S., Schutzstaffel, under Heinrich Himmler.

I don't know what my companions were thinking, but I didn't like the situation I was in. I could see my poor mother nearby, tearing her hair and crying. My father was talking to the elders, seeking my release—cajoling, bribing, pleading, begging, all to no avail. We were ordered to line up in rows of four. One of the S.A. yelled, *"Muetzen auf. Ruhe still gestanden"* (Attention. Stand quietly.) and recounted us 200 ablebodied men.

He reported to his superior. They saluted with a "Heil

Hitler" and ordered us to march out. Our four columns began to move, each of us carrying his luggage. The S.A. men flanked us, guns loaded and ready to shoot anyone who tried to escape. Our parents walked beside us, many crying helplessly. It was to be the last time I saw my mother and father.

We were marched to the main railway station, where a member of the Jewish Board of Elders gave us each ten "Zuban" cigarettes and made a speech: "You are pioneers," he said. "You are the first Jews to work for the German Reich. You will show the Germans that Jews are able and willing to work.

"In three months, you will be replaced by other Jews, and you will return home. In exchange for your labors, your relatives will be left in peace and their possessions and businesses will not be taken from them."

My feeling at this time was resentment and bitterness toward our leaders in the Jewish community.

My three months was to last until April 30, 1945. For many of my companions, the duration was to be shorter, ending with their deaths.

At noon, a train pulled into the station. It looked as if it had not been in use since World War I. We were counted again and loaded aboard, fifty prisoners and four guards to each car. I put my case under a bench in the compartment I shared with four other laborers and settled down, exhausted from all the excitement. The old steam engine started puffing. A whistle announced its departure. As we pulled out of the station, the heavens began to sob. I could see my mother watching nervously, as if she knew she was seeing her firstborn son off for the last time. I could hear the click-clack-click of the wheels as we pulled away. The rain poured down, accompanied by thunder and lightning. The whole world seemed darkened at that day, that hour, that minute.

I fell into a deep sleep as the train moved at its normal speed of about thirty miles per hour toward the unknown, toward Germany.

Shopping district where my father had his butcher shop

Castle in our town, built in approximately the eleventh century

Trade School "piast" that I attended during my apprenticeship as a plumber

Jewish High School of Fürstenberg

Jewish Old People's Home

Main Street in Bendzin, Malachowska

Railroad Station from which I left for the camps

The Yellow Building belonging to my grandparents

Grandpa Nathan, 1935

Grandma Rebecca and Cousin Fay during the German occupation (1940)

The man to the extreme right in this photo is Maurice, the plumbing contractor, who died in Buchenwald.

Uncle Tobias and his wife.
All of the family perished in Auschwitz.

Aunt Lola survived the camps. She died in Israel in 1979.

Uncle Abraham. All his family perished in Auschwitz.

*The Last of
the Numbered Men*

PART I: GROWING UP

Bendin

I was nineteen years old and on the way to an uncertain future, unable to visualize how things would develop. I didn't know if I would ever again see my home, my parents, my brothers; my large family of grandparents, uncles, aunts, and cousins. I knew only that I was on my own, having to take care of myself like a lost fawn in the forest. There was no choice: survival was the goal, endurance the game.

The town I was born in was in Poland, about seven miles from what was then the German border. The Poles called it Bedzin; the Germans, Bendsburg o/s (Oberschlesien—Upper Silesia); the Jews, Bendin. A Jewish settlement had existed there since the twelfth century. Jews constituted a majority of the town's population until after World War I and the bulk of its core until World War II.

For some, Bendin was full of life and prosperity, but there was also misery. Most of the Jewish population was very poor. The town was near the rich Silesian region of Germany in an area having an abundance of natural resources, but only a few could participate in that wealth. Bendin was a center of industry and commerce, with many independent, self-employed craftsmen: shoemakers, furniture manufacturers, and workers in all phases of the building industry. Jews took part in coal and iron mining and tin and zinc processing. Commerce in the inner city was all Jewish. Jews produced iron wire and nails, tools, and copper and aluminum wire, and had small "factories," making soap, candles, and paint. Even smaller shops produced everything from buttons to umbrellas. The garment industry was active and expanded steadily. However, few of these operations made their owners wealthy. Most were largely piecework operations, small sweatshops adjacent to the family's home, or in the home, which produced just marginal livings. For many, the workshop was the kitchen, and there the family also slept and ate, living from hand to mouth, making a few items and then taking them to market.

I remember Bendin in the 1930s, before hostilities began, as a brisk town, full of life, a clean city despite its poverty. It lay on the left bank of the river Black Przemsha. The right bank was farmland.

In 1931, it had a population of about 50,000, of which 24,000—48 percent—were Jewish. By 1939, 27,000—45 percent—of its 60,000 people were Jewish. An influx of Jews from outlying areas developed in the first years of the war, raising the Jewish population to 40,000 in 1941, but, by 1943, slaughter and shipment to camps had brought the Jewish population, for all practical purposes, to zero.

The inner city was almost completely Jewish. On the Sabbath, the area virtually closed. The street cars that traveled across town, which normally bustled with travelers, carried only the motorman and the conductor on Saturdays.

Bendin, being only about ten kilometers (six miles) from the German border, was heavily influenced by German culture. Its weekly markets attracted people from all the surrounding towns. Many Volksdeutsche—Poles of German ancestry—came to buy and sell. They browsed through booths set up in an area surrounded on three sides by the building containing shops that served our community throughout the week. The booths, of wood, were permanently set up in double rows and stood empty most of the time.

We Jews supported and were supported by a whole range of institutions. These included a Jewish home for the aged, the Jewish orphanage and a nonprofit loan organization supported by the Jewish Joint Committee of the United States. We had social organizations for art, music, culture, and physical education. There were a Jewish high school, a Hebrew high school, and two Jewish grade schools, one for boys and one for girls. A newspaper called *Zaglembier* was published each Friday.

About 5 percent of our people were considered wealthy. Another 15 percent were merchants and were considered middle class, and about 30 percent managed to make a living. The remaining 50 percent lived off the first half. They were not called poor; the word for them was "miserable."

My early years were relatively uneventful. I was born December 24, 1921, in a two-room apartment on the fourth floor of a building about a mile from my father's butcher shop at the marketplace. I was delivered at home by a midwife, as my two brothers would be in later years. There were no sanitary facilities or running water in our building. A pump on the ground level supplied water for cooking and drinking. For washing and laundry, water was brought from the river, 300 yards away. In winter, when the pump froze, we had to boil the river water for drinking. There were six outhouses for eighteen tenants. These were cleaned once a week, for the Sabbath.

Our apartment consisted of about 100 to 120 square feet of floor space, divided into a kitchen and another, all-purpose, area. My growing family slept in both rooms.

When I was five, I began attending a *kindergarten* for four hours each day. When I was seven, my father, David, accompanied me to my first-grade school, about three miles from our apartment. After that first trip, I was on my own, walking both ways daily.

My brother Jack was born in 1924, and Sam in 1929. As they grew, the apartment became too crowded, and in 1930 our parents decided to move to larger quarters. We used a horse and buggy to move.

The new apartment was grand, by our standards. While it was also only two rooms, it had nearly four times more floor space than we had had. It was on a second floor, only about half a block from Father's store. Best of all, it had a balcony that overlooked the street and that, in summer, became a third room. There I would study and, in the most stifling weather, sleep. The apartment was bright and cheerful, with sunlight reflecting readily from the red-painted wooden floors that my mother, Gitel, waxed each Friday.

The larger of the rooms was heated by a big ceramic stove. It had two closets and three beds, a table with six chairs at which we ate our Sabbath meal, and a sofa on which Father napped. A large wall clock rang out the hours.

Mother cooked on a wood- and coal-burning stove in the kitchen, and most of our meals were eaten at the kitchen table. For the dishes, there was a large wooden credenza and for my parents a double bed.

My parents both came from large families, so our lives included many aunts, uncles, and cousins. Mother had five sisters and two brothers. One of Father's brothers was killed in the Polish revolution, but four other brothers and three sisters remained. For much of the time, one or another of the aunts lived with us, helping mother and filling out our household.

Father worked very hard to make ends meet, often leaving home before 4:00 A.M. and returning as late as midnight. I saw him only on the Sabbath—Friday evening and Saturdays at lunch.

The new apartment, like the old, did not have running water, and Father took us three boys to a public bathhouse every Friday for a steambath and shower. At that time, we got a change of underwear, which we wore until the next Friday. Mother, in our absence, did her own bathing at home. When we men came back, we all dressed to go to the Temple for services. Mother would bless the Sabbath candles, cry, and make her secret wishes, probably asking God that our family should stay healthy and together.

My papa was a religious, devoted Jew, who sometimes missed meals because he had to delay his morning prayers. His favorite plea was "My God, let me die in my own bed." We didn't, then, appreciate what that prayer meant.

My life settled into a quiet pattern. I would wake and go

to school, walking the miles carrying my lunch, usually a kaiser roll with cheese. In the afternoon was religious school, then dinner, homework, and sleep. Often the afternoon also included time to play with the other boys at *Chedar*—Hebrew school.

In that summer of 1930, and the two that followed, we broke the pattern with a visit to my mother's father's farm. We would prepare for weeks to travel the thirty miles to the small village where grandpa lived and where my mother had been born, and we looked forward to the idle barefoot days spent swimming in the pond and playing in the forest. We helped with the animals and the chores. Sometimes, as a treat, we cooked outdoors over open flames, burying potatoes we had dug up in the coals to heat, like a hidden treat that came after our other food was ready.

At the age of eleven I enrolled into the choir in the great synagogue, where I sang for about eighteen months (until my voice changed) under the great cantor of the time, Mr. Supowitz. My parents were very proud of me.

Our fellow-Poles made life difficult. We were second-class citizens, heckled and boycotted by our non-Jewish countrymen.

The Polish government in the thirties had an official policy of harassing Jewish establishments. It strongly suggested that they be boycotted. The government blamed all its problems on the Jews.

Polish anti-Semitism was deep rooted. When a child misbehaved, his bogeyman was evoked by a motherly "I am going to call for the Jew."

The Jews were law-abiding citizens who were taxed beyond their ability to pay. Some lived without furniture for years because it was taken for back taxes. Only the really big businesses kept books, and everyone else paid based on exaggerated tax-collector estimates.

In 1934, I graduated from public school. I also became a Bar Mitzvah. In the Jewish faith, I was a man, able to be counted toward the quorum needed for public prayer. I was given my first long pants for the occasion. I read the Torah and delivered a speech during services. We had a party at our home for all the congregants. I was on my way to taking part in the life of our little community.

The next day, my father took me for a walk and an honest man-to-man talk.

"What do you want to do with your life?" Papa asked.

I knew he expected me to say, "I will work with you in the butcher shop," but I couldn't do it. I had never taken a liking to working with meat.

I asked Papa if I could continue school. He answered no, for the simple reason that he couldn't afford it. High school was private and costly. Even public school was not free and, with two other sons going to grade school and, in the afternoons, to Hebrew school, the budget was stretched thin.

Since high school was out of the question, I told Papa I would like my Uncle Maurice, who was a plumbing contractor, to teach me how to be a plumber. In the back of my mind, I was planning to leave Poland at the first opportunity and go to Palestine, and I knew that only in the building trades would I be able to make a living.

Papa disliked asking for favors but, in this instance, he promised that on the next Sabbath he would take me to my uncle and talk with him about taking me as an apprentice.

At that time, to be accepted into a trade, you had to pay the contractors. Work in any of the trades was scarce. Generally, sons, and especially the eldest, followed in their father's footsteps. I wanted to be an exception. It looked like a quiet rebellion, and I was pleased by Papa's promise. It was a first step in the direction I wanted to go.

That week was filled with anticipation. Being finished with school, I had much free time, which I used to go swimming in the river, to play soccer with the boys, or to dream and to worry.

How will it be? I wondered. *Will I be accepted? Will my dream come true? Will I be capable?* I knew plumbing would be hard work, but how hard?

Finally, it was Saturday. After lunch, our big meal, Papa

asked, "Are you ready, son?" I said yes, and off we went to Uncle Maurice and Aunt Lola's house.

It took us about ten minutes to get there. We arrived, greeted our hosts, and sat down. Then Papa started asking all kinds of questions. The answers—the whereabouts of uncles, aunts, and cousins—seemed interminable. I thought they had forgotten I was present and that Papa didn't have the guts to ask about my apprenticeship. My hands were wet from nervousness.

After an hour of listening, I was ready to give up. I stood. Father, getting the message quickly, changed the subject. "Would you please take my son as an apprentice?" he asked, looked at his sister as if to say, "I need your help. Would you please help me?"

Uncle Maurice answered, "Give me a week to think it over, and I'll let you know."

The next week was even longer than the last. Finally, on Friday, Aunt Lola stopped by Father's shop to say I should come with him Saturday afternoon for coffee and cake. I had a sleepless night, but, as the time to visit neared, I became more confident. I told myself that, if worse came to worst, I could always become a butcher.

So, after lunch on Saturday, off we went. The smile on Aunt Lola's face when we arrived said. "You'll be accepted." We all greeted each other and sat down for the promised cake and coffee. I had milk—I didn't drink coffee yet—and listened to more talk about uncles, aunts, and cousins.

At last, Uncle Maurice got up and stood before me. "So you want to be a plumber?" he asked.

I hadn't lost my powers of speech, but I just nodded, yes.

Then he gave a speech on the difficulty of being an apprentice. There would be twelve-hour days and no pay for three years, until I was a journeyman. I would work six days a week, including Sunday, when the shop was closed, cleaning the tools for the regular week.

I accepted all terms.

Papa didn't like the whole thing. I was thirteen, and he

would have to support me completely until I was sixteen and could earn my way. Regardless, it was decided, and I became the third apprentice in my uncle's company. I was to report Monday at 7:00 A.M. sharp. That first day I arrived at 6:15, the first to enter the shop. I was assigned to Frank, a strong, tall fellow of German heritage, very precise and punctual. The first weeks, he worked my butt off. Gradually, I grew to understand his language, which was rough and mean. Once he said to me, "Either you'll become a good mechanic or you'll go sell onions in the market." After we had worked together for one year, he invited me out for a beer after work. It was his silent acceptance of me into the family of plumbers.

We traveled to nearby towns doing plumbing and sewer work. Our labors were hard in those days before electrical tools. All digging for sewers was done by hand, even in stone. Hammer, chisel, and shovel were our only tools. However, it felt good to produce something with your hands for your fellowman.

During the second year of my apprenticeship, I still did most of my work under Frank's watchful eye. I mastered the trade well because I knew this was the way I would earn a living for the rest of my life.

Four times a week I went to evening classes at trade school. These lasted two or three hours, depending on the day. There were no classes on Fridays, Saturdays and Sundays. I moved into line to run my own projects with a helper or more junior apprentice, but I was not to get an assignment until the end of my second year.

At home, Papa used to tease me. When I worked outside laying sewers, he used to say when I came home: "Look at you. You wanted to become a miner, not earning any money." He had to buy me shoes and overalls for work. I did all kinds of chores—bringing in coal for the oven, chopping wood, bringing in groceries, babysitting, going to the library to change books—so I could earn a quarter for a ticket for the movies.

In the meantime, life became more difficult. Anti-Semitism sprang up like mushrooms after a rain. Germany came under the dictatorship of Adolph Hitler. His speeches reached our area with its large German population. The Poles were good disciples for his message about the Jews, which reinforced their own basic bias. The German government capitalized actively on this, recruiting many for a fifth column in Poland, which would become active if Germany moved to take over its neighbor, which eventuality the government knew was only a matter of time.

In 1935, when Josef Pilsudski, the leader of the Polish revolution, died, we knew changes would occur and not for the better. A clique of colonels took over the government. Poland was a feudal country with one of the worst standards of living in Europe. About 30 percent of the population was illiterate. New laws were passed to suppress the Jewish merchants. Every economic ill was blamed on the Jews. A new anti-Semitic party, the National Democratic Party, came into being. We called them NDKS. In schools, segregation was enforced. In advanced academic schools, "Numerus Clausus"—a quota—was introduced. Only 2 or 3 percent of the students could be Jewish, and they had to sit on the last benches in class.

In various parts of the country, skirmishes occurred which sometimes turned into pogroms in which Jews lost their property and their lives and Jewish women were raped. Jews were not free to walk the streets, especially at night. Our resentment was at a boiling point, but there wasn't much we could do.

In 1936, my younger brother, Jack, graduated from public school and joined Papa in the butcher shop. This made things much better in the shop and at home. Life became more comfortable and relaxed for us, and, to make things even better, in the middle of 1937, I became a journeyman plumber. New horizons opened for me.

To Palestine

Finally I was earning my own way, being paid by my uncle for my labor. I was a good plumber, and it now seemed that my dream of going to Palestine could be made a reality. A friend of mine, Isaak, who was two years my senior, and I decided to emigrate illegally. Without our parents' knowledge, we studied maps and prepared ourselves. I knew that Papa would never allow me to leave, as he firmly believed that we should wait for the Messiah to bring us forth into the promised land of our forefathers.

After our decision, it took me several months to accumulate 100 zlotys (about $20) from my earnings to finance my way. At that time, 100 zlotys would support a family of four for about a month. A laborer earned one or two zlotys a day. Money in hand, we were ready to leave. Our plan was to go through Czechoslovakia and Austria to Italy and stow away on a ship to Haifa or Jaffa.

We headed to the railroad station, where I mailed a letter to my parents, and left for the Czech border. Without passports, we couldn't cross the border on the train, so, in the evening, when we reached the Polish frontier, we disembarked and waited until about eleven o'clock at night to move ahead on foot.

We crossed near Sol and walked for about two hours. We weren't quite sure what direction we were headed in, but we knew we had left Poland when we overheard the border guards talking a language similar to, but different from, Polish.

By morning, we reached a village. We weren't sure what to do. The farmers were already at work in their fields. We didn't have Czechoslovakian money, and our speech would immediately mark us as foreign. We were in a predicament.

We decided to wait until evening and try our luck at the farms. We spent the day resting in the fields of the trackless countryside.

Toward dusk, we approached the first farmhouse we came to and asked, in Polish, if we could sleep there. Our languages were similar enough for us to be understood. We found out we were about fifteen kilometers—almost ten miles—from the border, and to catch a train we would have to walk twenty more kilometers. The only daily train for Prague left at three o'clock in the afternoon.

The farm family was friendly, giving us potatoes, bread, and pork, and telling us to sleep in the barn and leave in the morning.

At about midnight, however, two Czech border police appeared in the barn and told us to get up and follow them on foot. I didn't know how they had found out about us, but we couldn't argue. They were on bicycles, which they rode slowly so we could keep up.

We went to the station on the Czech side of the border, where we were questioned about our plans. They seemed to think we were thieves or vandals and questioned us intermittently through an interpreter for the next few hours. Alternately, they asked questions and left us alone to sweat it out. We told them our plans, showing them the red pencil marks on our map and telling them where we were headed and why.

At eight o'clock, an officer of the guard arrived. The guards reported the two criminals they had caught, and we were questioned for another two hours. Then they gave us coffee, escorted us across Niemandsland (No-man's land), and turned us over to the Polish border police.

The Poles were less polite than the Czechs. They stripped us to look for our well-hidden traveling funds, and grilled us for hours about our plan.

At five o'clock, they took us by train to Zywiec, the nearest town with a magistrate and jail. Since we arrived about six, the court was already closed. We were locked up with notorious criminals to await morning. It became one of the longest nights Isaak and I had ever spent. We lay awake on flea-infested blankets, watching the other inmates going through our clothes looking for the money the guards had been unable to find.

At 9:00 A.M., the guards who had brought us to jail escorted us to court. The judge asked us the same questions we had already answered on both sides of the border, and we repeated our responses.

I added that since the Poles preached that the Jews should go to Palestine, we had only been trying to oblige. "You shouldn't punish us, you should help us," I said.

The judge deliberated for about an hour before sentencing us to thirty days in jail and one year's probation for crossing the border illegally. Because I was a minor, however, he suspended my jail term. Isaak had to spend the thirty days in prison.

I left the courtroom, and let the fresh air wash away the nightmare of the last three days. I went to a secluded corner, where I opened the seam at the collar of my jacket and removed the tightly folded 100-zloty note that my uncle Baruch, a tailor, had sewn there for me. The memory of the guards and the criminals holding the jacket, their hands on the collar containing the bill as they searched the pockets and linings, provided my one bright memory since our capture.

I bought enough food and tobacco to last Isaak until he was released and made up a nice package for him. I brought it to the jail guards for inspection, and it was delivered to him in my presence. We exchanged a few words and I headed to the railroad station, where I bought a ticket on the next train to Bendin.

I arrived home late in the evening. Mama opened the door and almost fainted when she saw my condition. She made me undress in the vestibule outside our door and leave my clothes outside. She warmed water, and I took a hot bath, washing for about an hour to drown any lingering vermin. I started to tell her what had happened to me, but she interrupted, telling me to go to bed and tell my story the next day when everyone was up. The rest of the family had already gone to bed before I arrived, Mama having stayed up to finish her chores.

It was almost noon when I woke. Breakfast was on the table, and probably had been for hours. I washed and dressed while mother waited patiently for me to relate my experiences.

I took the rest of the week off, visiting relatives and looking for a new job at higher pay. There were no unions then, and you worked for what the market could bear. I found a contractor who offered me twenty zlotys a week, double what my uncle paid me. I took the job.

By the time Isaak returned home a month later, I had settled into my work routine. He went back to his job as a butcher, and we did not again try to head for Palestine.

About three months after my return, a Mr. Sapinsky knocked at our door and asked for me. He told me he had gotten the job of bringing sewer and water facilities into our building under a law requiring all landlords to connect their buildings to the town's new sewer and water systems and to provide public toilets in the basement for all tenants. He said he had heard I was a good plumber and asked if I were interested in doing that job for him. There would be other jobs, too, as long as I wanted to work for him. He offered to pay me forty-eight zlotys a week!

The figure hit me like a thunderbolt, but there was one catch: I had to work six hours each Saturday, a great difficulty since my father was very religious and observed the Sabbath strictly. However, the salary was too good to pass up. I agreed to take the job.

I took Mama into my confidence, explaining what was at stake, and with her help I would sneak out Saturday mornings, dressed up, then change to my working clothes at that week's project.

The new job made life a little bit easier, providing a measure of luxury. When I received my first week's salary, I was like a child. I took the zloty notes and stopped in all the shops, buying fresh fruit and other treats and filling my pockets with the jingling change. With my pants bulging, I felt like the tallest man on the earth.

The second week, I bought a beautiful Swiss watch, which I looked at constantly, as much to check its reality as the time. I could finally afford to buy new clothes and to go places I couldn't even have thought about before.

I worked for Mr. Sapinsky for about eight months. Our apartment got running water and a sink, and I even laid out a place for a toilet, but I never did put it in, because we needed the space for a bed.

War Clouds

By 1938, Germany had been joined by Poland and Hungary in taking over parts of Czechoslovakia. Dark clouds had started to form in the European sky. The Germans acquired the Sudetenland, which had a German population of about 3 million. The Anschluss of Austria in March of 1938 brought another 10 million people of German ancestry under Hitler's control.

Poland participated in the partitioning of Czechoslovakia, acquiring the district of Teshin with its 230,000 inhabitants, 130,000 of them Czechs. That decision was to prove costly for Poland, making it more vulnerable when Germany turned on it months later.

The Russians sought permission to go through Poland to help the Czechs, but this was flatly refused by the Poles through their Foreign Minister, who was rumored to be a German sympathizer.

In November, a Jewish refugee from Germany, upset by deportation, killed the third secretary of the German embassy in Paris. This led to "spontaneous" demonstrations against Jews throughout Germany. This so-called *"Kristallnacht,"* or "Night of Broken Glass," was named for the millions of marks' worth of glass shattered at the hundreds of synagogues, shops, and dwellings destroyed in the rampage that marked the start in earnest of the pogroms that were to continue until Hitler's death. Flames lit the skies of Germany. Women and children were shot or otherwise injured as they sought to escape the fires. Thousands of Jews were arrested and sent to concentration camps.

The Jews of Bendin organized a massive protest march in reaction to the horrors of the *Kristallnacht*. About 5,000 people marched to the county seat. There, the president of the Jewish community delivered a written protest to be sent to the German government. We protesters dispersed in silence, returning to what remained of our normal lives. There was little else we could do, except clasp our fists in anger and disgust.

German Jews of Polish origin were being deprived of their material goods by order of the German government. They were assembled at the railroad stations for deportation with twenty pounds of belongings and ten marks (about four dollars) in cash. Our townspeople took in and cared for about 2,000 of these unfortunates, giving them shelter and providing jobs for those able to work.

Winter set in early in 1938. Life was difficult, but most people still hoped for a better tomorrow. For many, that winter meant unbearable cold and scarcely any food on the table.

Anti-Semitism continued to be fashionable. Jews were beaten daily. Incidents sometimes turned into riots or small pogroms. No Jew in any Polish town could be sure of his or her life.

By March, 1939, Hitler had annexed what was left of Czechoslovakia and installed a puppet regime in Bohemia and Moravia, completely eliminating the last truly democratic state in eastern Europe. We could feel in our bones what was coming next, as Hitler, in his speeches and published statements, sought a new era, demanding a corridor through Poland to unite Germany and the city of Danzig in East Prussia.

In our home, life was uneventful. Mother prepared for spring cleaning, painting and washing our apartment for Passover. I became an independent contractor, working with Leo, a soccer player in our class-A league. I was ecstatic when we signed our first contract, with a Polish teacher by the name of Stanek to put plumbing in his building. We finished in August, 1939, after three months' work.

Around us, that summer, things were getting hotter by the day, if not by the hour. The pressure from the Germans was unbelievable. The German Embassy in Warsaw organized Poles of German ancestry and financed local Polish "patriots," like the NDKS, who were extremely anti-Semitic. And, as the horror mounted, the Polish Parliament (Sejm and Senate) discussed whether the government should allow ritual slaughter of animals. What irony!

As the Germans massed troops on the Polish border, from the Baltic to areas that were formerly Czechoslovakia, mass meetings were held in sport stadiums with speakers declaring that we Poles wouldn't give the Germans even a button (just a whole coat).

We would hear over the radio the speeches of the "Fuehrer," and experience told us that nothing was likely to save Poland from disaster. The only hope was an existing guarantee of mutual assistance from France and England. The question was whether they would honor it.

BLITZKRIEG IN POLAND

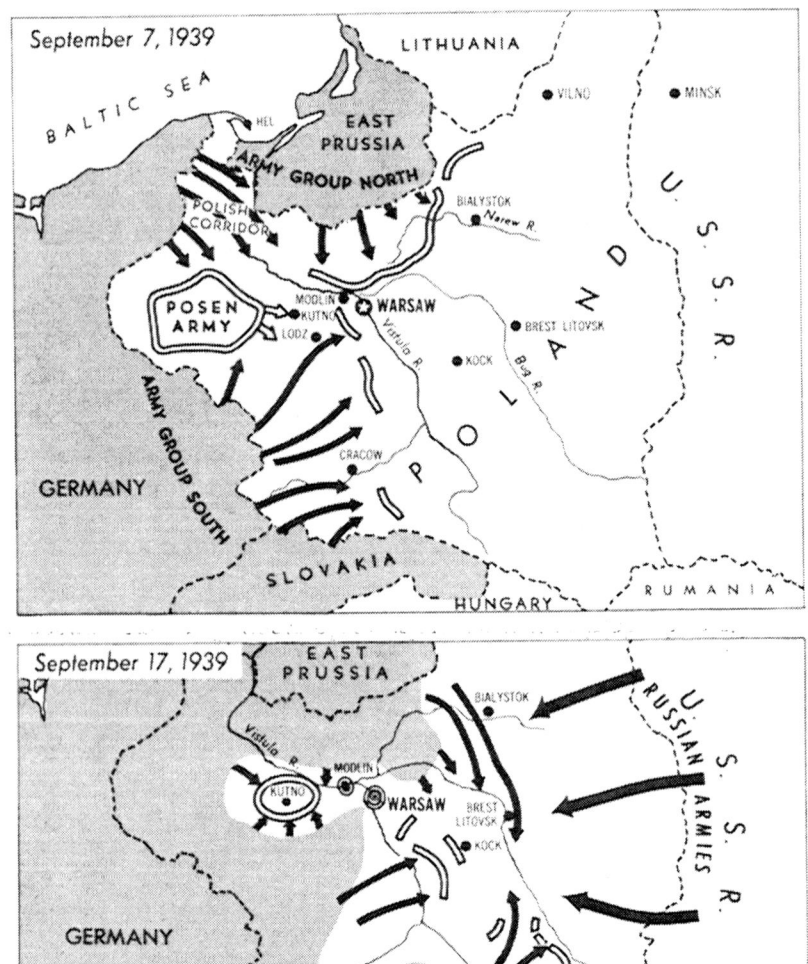

From *Military History of World War II*, Vol. 1, *European Land Battles 1939–1943,* by Trevor Nevitt Dupuy (New York, Franklin Watts).

From *Military History of World War II,* Vol. 1, *European Land Battles 1939–1943,* by Trevor Nevitt Dupuy (New York, Franklin Watts).

War

On August 31, 1939, German radio announced that Polish soldiers had fired on German territory. Men in Polish army uniforms attacked a radio station near Gleiwitz, a town in Upper Silesia near the Polish border, and broadcast in Polish a call for Poland to attack Germany. In fact, the attackers were S.S. (Shutzstaffel) troops in Polish uniforms under orders to create an incident to give Germany an excuse to invade Poland and set World War II into full motion.

The S.S. had become a state within a state, and from 1933 to 1945 was charged, among other things, with exterminating in Germany and, later, the whole of Europe, every Jewish man, woman, and child.

Incident in hand: Germany invaded the nation of Poland on September 1.

News of the invasion dominated the airwaves that Friday, and I decided to enlist to fight the Nazis. Without telling anyone, I went to the outskirts of Bedzin, where the 23rd Artillery Regiment was stationed, to volunteer. I said a mental goodbye to my parents and brothers, whom I might never see again. I was eighteen. They would never have agreed to my enlistment and would have done everything to prevent it—even chain me to my bed—in order that the family might share its destiny together.

After signing up, I took my civilian clothes to my former boss, Mr. Sapinsky, who lived near regimental headquarters, and asked him to bring them and a note to my parents so they'd know where I'd gone.

The sergeant who accepted me took me to the firing range and taught me to shoot and clean a rifle. The lesson lasted an hour. Then, in uniform but without even having dogtags, I left on foot with the last of the troops. I was a soldier without a name; they called me "the volunteer from Bedzin."

We marched day and night as the army's units were dispersed in the chaos of the first days of war.

We watched the skies, looking for our air force to support us. When planes appeared, our troops cheered, yelling *"Nasze"* (ours), but they turned out to be German Stukas, spraying death from machine guns on anything that moved. Poland's air force had been destroyed by the Luftwaffe on the first day of fighting, though we didn't find this out until after many men were killed.

During one of the air attacks, I found myself near the captain of the 20th Infantry Regiment. With Stukas sweeping overhead, I saluted him. He briskly ordered me to get under cover and to stay close to him. He kept me under his protection, and I finally had a place in the army, as his adjutant.

The roads over which we moved as we went east, away from Germany, to regroup for battle, were crowded with civilians fleeing their homes with all they could carry. Some were in horse-drawn buggies, some pulled carts, some had their possessions on their backs.

We marched twenty or thirty kilometers to a railway depot, where we were given travel preference because of our guns. We boarded and headed farther east, relieved to be off the roads, where we had also been prey to German fifth columnists. These Nazis in Polish uniforms would sneak up on straggling soldiers at night, choke them with steel wire, and drag them off the road.

On the train, too, there was danger, though not to soldiers. I was in a compartment with several civilians, including a priest and Jew. Three or four of the men were harassing the Jew and finally decided to throw him from the moving train.

I appealed to the priest for help, but he couldn't do a thing, and the Jew was tossed from the car's door. Those Poles were truly ripe for Hitler's plans. Even while being chased by the Germans, they still had time to harass Jews.

About 200 kilometers from the border, the train came to a halt. The rails ahead had been destroyed by bombing, and it could go no farther. We soldiers got off and joined with other regiments to form a last-ditch defensive line.

At the start of the German invasion, Poland had a regular army of 600,000 men and reserves of two million, which were never called up. Its air force, some 500 planes, had ceased to exist as a fighting force within twenty-four hours of the first battle.

The partitioning of Czechoslovakia was quickly revealed as another German ploy and a great disadvantage to Poland. German holdings from that action enabled it to attack from the south as well as the west and north.

The Polish army fought bravely, but, without planes and beset from all sides, including from the long-established fifth column within itself, it could not last long. The Germans bombed at will. Poland's General Headquarters was attacked, and our troops were unable to get directions and information on enemy—and our own—movements. Lack of coordination and daily air attacks created confusion in all our defenses. We made a few stands but largely without success. We were fighting World War I–style battles, using horses, while Germany fought a Blitzkrieg with armor, tanks and mechanized half-tracks.

Our troops made an all-out effort to stand against the Germans in Alexandrow, Josefow and Janow Lubelski. We had about 17,000 soldiers but were encircled by the Germans. We were ordered to fight with rifles against tanks. Anyone retreating was shot by his own officers. I thought the situation was ridiculous and hopeless, and I questioned the impulse that had led me on this adventure, but I fought on. The battle went on for three days, with many casualties. I fired all my ammunition and was left with an empty rifle and a bayonet with which to face machine guns and artillery.

At this point, I found myself in a foxhole with a Ukrainian from an area ceded to Poland after World War I. We became fighting pals, each of us wondering what he was doing there, and feeling somewhat ridiculous.

The outcome of the battle and, indeed, of the war, was never in doubt. No matter how bravely the Polish army fought, its soliders were only fodder for German tanks and artillery. Those who survived that onslaught became targets for German planes.

England and France had declared war on Germany on September 3. That news had filled us with joy. We thought the French army would march into the Rhineland from the west and the French air force would be sent to help us. However, this didn't happen. While fighting raged in Poland, French soldiers sat along their fortified Maginot line, either unwilling or unable to help. England also did nothing to help the Poles. It was a Munich conference of a different style.

On September 18, a general spoke to us. "We are surrounded by Germans, and there is no way out," he declared. "Yesterday, the Russian Army invaded Poland from the east, and we are between two advancing armies." The Polish army was paralyzed and in full disarray. The next day, the general staff fled to Romania.

The Ukrainian and I decided we were now on our own. As the battle continued, we found a pair of fallen medics. We put on their red-cross armbands and took their stretcher and carried wounded to a field hosptal behind the lines. After several trips, we left the hospital and headed in separate directions toward our homes.

I was about 500 kilometers from Bendin. I was unsure how to get there, but I decided to start by walking to the nearest village, which was called Bilgoray. It was dark when I arrived. I could hear German artillery pounding not far away. I stopped at one Jewish household, where I told them I was a Jew and asked for clothes and a place to sleep. They refused out of fear.

Finally I found a Polish family who took me in. They knew only that I was a Polish soldier. I sought civilian clothes so I could go back home. In uniform, I knew, I was marked as a target, and I was terrified of being taken prisoner by the Germans. The family gave me a jacket and a pair of pants. I buried my rifle and bayonet. Perhaps, someday, someone would make use of them, I thought.

That night I slept like a dead man, making up, in part, for many sleepless nights at the front. In the morning, my Polish host told me the bad news: the Germans were in town. I wasn't surprised but I was scared speechless, expecting the worst from the invaders.

I had no choice but to leave. Nobody wanted to keep or hide an ex-soldier. All were afraid of being punished by the victors. Before setting out, I gathered my courage and went to the center of the village to see what the enemy looked like. There was a victory parade, which lasted about an hour. Nobody was on foot. Column after mechanized column passed. Motorcycles with sidecars carried up to three soliders each. Half-tracks and full-tracks brought up the rear. Then an S.S. unit stopped in the middle of town, set up its field kitchen, and ordered all shops and stores to open. The S.S. did not participate in battle. They followed the army, occupied conquered communities and terrorized, maimed, and killed civilians to keep the subjugated populace under control.

At Bilgoray, the S.S. went on a "shopping" spree, taking whatever caught their fancy without saying a word.

Homeward Bound

I had seen enough. I decided to leave immediately for home. I still wore the heavy military boots I had received as a volunteer, but I wore my pants legs over them to disguise the appearance that I had been a soldier.

After about three hours, I stopped at the side of the road to rest. While I sat, a horse and wagon appeared. I stopped the driver and asked where he was headed. He said he was going toward Katovic, which was sixteen kilometers from Bendin.

"Will you take me with you?" I asked.

"How much money do you have?" he returned.

"About five zlotys."

"I can't take you for that little," he said.

I was desperate, so I offered him my watch, the Swiss-made 17-jeweled Tissot I had bought with my early earnings. I didn't want to part with it, but I wanted even less to walk 500 kilometers. He took it, and we were on our way.

After about two hours, we were stopped by S.A.—stormtroopers. They said all ablebodied males had to help restore a bridge that had been destroyed by the retreating Polish army. My host, in fluent German, told the soliders he was of German ancestry and had an ulcer and couldn't work. He was allowed to drive on while I was taken to join the 80 to 100 men pressed into working on the bridge. He waved farewell, my watch on his left wrist. I was near tears.

The bridge work was going on night and day. I worked

until dusk, when I excused myself for an errand of nature. I walked away into the bushes and hid. When night fell, I slipped away.

That night, I slept soundly under the sky. I was so exhausted by the war that I couldn't even worry about my plight. The first light of morning woke me. The river was nearby, so I took off my clothes and bathed. I was afraid to walk before full daylight because I knew the Germans had imposed a curfew of 10:00 P.M. to 6:00 A.M. for all Poles and 7:00 P.M. to 7:00 A.M. for Jews.

When I figured it was past 7:00, I took off my boots, which were uncomfortable after I had slept in them, and started walking. My destination was the town of Kielce, about 100 kilometers from where I had left the army.

As I walked, I passed little villages with Jewish populations, where I saw for the first time the "Master Race" at work. Its rage was aimed mainly at Jews. On the eve of Yom Kippur, I reached Opatow Lagow, where I took refuge with the shamus (caretaker) of the synagogue. I spent that holy day in his house, sitting and meditating, reviewing what had happened and what was happening. Outside, the Germans were abusing the citizenry. Jews with beards were easily recognized and persecuted. Anti-Jewish violence was no different from the violence that would later be directed at the Poles, but the Jews came first, and, for the time being, the Poles could laugh.

Personally, I feared the Poles more than the Germans. The Poles were fundamentally anti-Semitic because of their zealous Christianity. Their violence stemmed from their desire for Jews to embrace Christianity and from the doctrine that blamed the Jews for Christ's death.

Horrible terror reigned in those first days of German occupation. Innocent people were taken captive or shot on sight. After the Wehrmacht, the regular army, left, the S.D. (Sicherheits Dienst) the security arm of the S.S., arrived and terrorized everyone. Jews had to make special contributions to meet levies imposed by the S.S. In larger towns, the S.D. demanded kilos of gold and silver and confiscated all radios and furs. Hell was in full view. Even thirty-seven years after my liberation, I have trouble accepting the terrorism and oppression that took place. Polish earth was soaked with Jewish blood. In no other country could the Germans have done what they did there with the help of the Poles, Ukrainians, Lithuanians, and others. The worst of the extermination camps were in Poland. Educated and "cultured" people went on savage rampages and murdered innocent men, women, and children alike. It was as if God had taken a vacation. People were shot, hanged, beaten, and maimed simply for being Jewish.

After my day of meditation, I resumed my hike to Kielce. I decided to go the sixty kilometers from Opatow in one day, an ambitious course, which proved barely possible. After twelve hours of walking, with only a few ten-minute rest stops, I reached the outskirts of Kielce. It was none too soon. My legs had turned to wood; I couldn't feel them. I managed to find a place to sleep, with other refugees on the floor of a house.

Kielce, though smaller than Bendin, was still a major town, the seat of government for the area and a stop on the railroad.

When I woke up, I went to the center of the city to obtain a permit to travel home. Everybody had to get one if he were moving between towns. I was directed by a passerby to city hall, where two long lines had already formed, one for Jews and one for other Poles. I soon found out that Jews were being given only walking permits, good outside the twelve hours of curfew. The Poles could get passes to take the train. I got in the line for Poles.

I was only mildly apprehensive about passing as a non-Jew. I had blue eyes and brownish hair. I was concerned only about my nose, which I was afraid was not pointed enough.

After a tense two-hour wait, I came before a Polish clerk, who was sitting with a German who spoke Polish. I was asked my name.

"Henryk Posnanski," I replied, keeping my first name but making my last name more Polish.

"Father's name?"

"Stanislaw."
"Mother's name?"
"Eugenia."
May God forgive me for making my nice Jewish parents Polish and Christian, I thought.

My answers and accent were good enough to pass, and I was given papers permitting me to ride the train, good for six months from date of issue and allowing me to take three other persons—Poles, naturally—with me.

Pass in hand, I found three fellow-Jews from my own town and took them to the railroad station. On the platform, there were German soldiers with machine guns checking everybody. I produced my pass, which was in German with a big twisted cross imprinted on it. The soldier read it. One thing about the Germans: they respected papers. Everything had to be in order.

We were waved by and boarded the train for Katovic. The minute we sat down, we heard the Poles around us starting to talk among themselves. I could only hear the word "Jews," "Jews," "Jews," repeated, it seemed, over and over again. I was afraid, but I had to do something. Since the pass was in my assumed name, I felt responsible for the safety of my companions. I stood up and said I was Polish and had been in the army fighting for Poland and I had brought these three fellows with me because they were sick. This quieted our fellow travelers, but I still didn't trust them. I told my companions to disperse to different cars so as to be less obvious.

Finally, the train left the station. It was a relief to get rid of the German soldiers on the platform. I was among my fellow Poles. There was only one thing I didn't know: in order for the train to get to Katovic, we had to go through Germany proper. The direct line, from Jedziejow to Miechow had been bombed by the German Luftwaffe at the beginning of the war and was out of order. To get to Katovic, we had to go through ChenstochowaPruskie, Herby, Koenigsberg, and Beuten-Katovic. When we arrived at Chenstochowa, my three companions were too scared to continue the ride and left the train. I should have gone too, but I was not willing to walk another eighty kilometers to Bendin. I remembered my sixty-kilometer walk from Opatow to Kielce. Whatever would be, I was going through Germany to home. I figured I would take my chances, which, looking back, was very foolish.

We arrived in Koenigsberg after midnight. My stomach had began to hurt. I hadn't eaten all day and had eaten very little the days before. I took a walk toward the station and found a snack bar. All I had in my pocket were two Polish zlotys, which were worthless in Germany. I mustered my courage and went to the bar to ask for bread. The girl behind the counter didn't understand my question because I was speaking Polish. Seeing I was getting nowhere, I started to ask in German, which is similar to Yiddish. Nearby, however, was a German conductor who, the minute I opened my mouth, exclaimed, *"Du bist ein Jude"* (You are a Jew). I answered, "Nein—no—I am Polish and on my way home." By sheer luck, he was suddenly called to the phone, saving me from a dangerous situation. The minute he left, I headed back to my train, trembling. All the trains and the station were blacked out because the war with France and England continued. I lay in the dark for about one hour before the train finally started moving.

The Poles on board made constant threats regarding what they intended to do to the Jews back home. My stomach turned as I listened to what they had on their minds.

At about 6:00 A.M., the train pulled into the next station, Beuten. I went inside, wanting only to stretch my legs. I had learned my lesson about speaking in Koenigsberg and avoided everyone.

Suddenly, there appeared in front of me a tall man with blond hair and blue eyes. I froze before this specimen of Aryan manhood. He looked at me and spoke calmly in perfect Hebrew, "Disappear if you don't want to be recognized. Cut off a piece of your nose." He was not threatening, just advising, but I was stunned by this Aryan Jew. I didn't wait to hear more. Turning with a thank-you and a goodbye, I walked briskly away from the station, terrified, never turning my head to look back.

It was a rainy day. German flags flew from every building.

The Germans greeted each other with Nazi salutes. Victory was theirs that day, and they were ecstatic. I took off my boots and started walking toward Katovic, eighteen kilometers away, where one of my uncles lived. It took me three hours to reach that next city.

Katovic was decked with flags, just as Beuten had been, and the people also saluted each other with outthrust arms. The difference was that these were Poles who had just become Germans and were more fanatical than Germans in their fervor. A chill went through me. Yesterday's Poles were today's Germans. I could visualize being in the Polish army with these guys choking their countrymen with thin steel wire in the middle of the night. Big banners hanging high across the main street proclaimed, *"Ein Gott, Ein Reich, Ein Fuehrer"* (one God, one country, one leader). I had had enough for one day. Quickly, I sought 23 Slowacka Street. I knocked on the door, but there was no answer. Like thousands of others, my uncle and his family had fled. I didn't give it much thought. I was only twelve kilometers from home, only a two-hour walk. With a shrug, I took off in the direction of Shopenitz-Sosnowitz-Bedzin.

After about forty-five minutes, I arrived at the bridge dividing Shopenitz and Sosnowitz. It had become a checkpoint since the Germans had moved their border eastward. My heart started to pound. I braced myself and faced the unavoidable. I joined the line to cross the bridge. Everybody was asked for identification. I produced my travel pass. An interpreter asked in Polish if I would be going back to Germany, since my pass was valid for six months. I answered no, so they took my pass and waved me along. With a sigh of relief, I continued on.

In another twenty minutes, I was in Sosnowitz, where another of my mother's sisters and her family lived. I was almost home. I reached their apartment, where I was greeted warmly. I had to tell them everything I had lived through in the previous three weeks. I washed up and ate a good meal, the first I'd had since I left home. I thanked them for the hospitality and went on, taking an electric streetcar to Bendin. As I rode, I thought about how to avoid shocking my parents with my return home. They might have given me up for dead already.

Twenty minutes later, I arrived home. It was before the big Jewish holiday Sukkoth, and my parents were both in the shop selling meat for the holiday to those who had German ration coupons. When I knocked at our apartment door, the aunt who was living with us opened it and almost fainted. When she came to, she started crying as if she'd seen a ghost. In a way, she had. There had been rumors that I was dead, fallen in the battle of Janow. Others said I was a prisoner-of-war in Lublin. My brother Sam went to the store to tell my parents that I was home and in one piece. The news quickly reached all my other relatives, who came, one by one, to greet and touch me and confirm that I was whole.

The scene when my parents came home was overwhelming. My mother cried hysterically. My father lectured me, telling me what a fool I was and what I had done to my mother's health. She hadn't slept at night, thinking of me lost or wounded somewhere. Father, my brothers, and I were given clean underwear and went to the public bath next to our building. It was so nice to take a real steambath, followed by a cold shower. We put on our clean clothes and went home. Mother had washed and dressed, and she looked like a queen in her own domain. Dinner was set. Father offered the holiday prayers as we participated silently. Public gatherings for any reason were strictly forbidden, and so we were to have our Sabbath services at home, in silence. Mother blessed the candles and cried, praying for all of us and for everyone in need of help from above. After prayers, we sat down and ate the meal she had lovingly prepared. When we finished, Papa again gave thanks to the Almighty. Then, everybody sat quietly, waiting for me to tell everything that had happened to me while I was away. I told my experiences in detail. Mother cried, perhaps with joy that the Almighty had returned her firstborn uninjured.

Bendsburg

When I finished speaking, there was a pause while my family considered what I had been through. Then they told me of their ordeal while I was gone.

On September 2, a few bombs had been dropped on Bedzin, but they caused no great damage. Many people, even the police, left as the German army advanced. Everyone feared the unknown. By September 3, the town was almost empty, open to the whim of the invader.

Everybody expected the worst. People bought what supplies they could, preparing for whatever was to be.

On September 4, the victorious Germans marched into Bedzin. They were greeted by Poles with flowers while the Jews stayed in their houses, afraid to go outside. The next day, the S.D. arrived in town. They immediately promulgated printed orders restricting everybody and everything, especially Jews. No more than three people could assemble at any time, at any place. Jews were not allowed to assemble for any activity, including prayer. By September 6, terror was being unleashed to its fullest. The Germans took two notable Jewish bakers and hanged them in public on a charge of overcharging 0.01 zloty for a loaf of bread that cost half a zloty. Everyone had to come and watch the good work done. On September 8, the S.D. assembled all the men from Berek Joselewitz Street, a major Jewish area, on the River Bridge, where they were beaten and thrown into the river. Whoever managed to swim to safety was shot. This was small game for the Germans, like fox-hunting.

On September 9, the Germans, with the help of local Poles, burned down the most beautiful synagogue in Poland. Fifty occupied Jewish apartments surrounding the synagogue were also set afire. The area was cordoned off, and anyone trying to escape the flames was shot. Several hundred Jews perished, either by fire or German bullets. About 100 of these people were burned beyond recognition and had to be buried in a mass grave in the Jewish cemetery.

The terror did not let up. The next day, they took all the men from Pilsudski Street—seventeen in total—shot them, and buried them during the night in the Polish cemetery. The burial was a blasphemy, which struck deeply at the sensibilities of the Jewish community. The German actions were not only a physical horror; they were a psychological terror, premeditated and formulated with German precision to bring the Jewish population of Bedzin under brute control. This control was exercised directly by German *"Treuhaender"* (trustees) who, within days of the invasion, took over all the factories, shops and larger enterprises in Bendin. Smaller shops and stores were taken over later.

The fear engendered by the S.D. was so great that many Jews, especially religious men who were easily recognizable by their beards and side locks, avoided the street.

Food lines became a way of life. Generally, young girls were sent to get bread and meat. Poles pointed Jews out to the Germans, and they were thrown out of line and sent off emptyhanded, often after they had waited for hours. Life became unbearable, and it was only the beginning.

Bedzin, which had been among the cleanest cities in Poland, became an eyesore—a collage of half-finished public works, burned-out ruins, empty shops, and people in tattered clothes.

Anyone found on the streets in our neighborhood was liable to be stopped and searched by the Shutzpolizei—the municipal police, called "Shupo" for short. Especially feared was a Shupo named Mitchke, a former middleweight champion prizefighter in Silesia, who often administered a beating with his body searches.

Somehow, the will to survive, to outlive the persecutors, remained strong. Though life had become joyless and humiliating for the average Jew, we hoped for the day of reckoning.

All basic commodities were rationed. Naturally, a black market developed, with prices hiked ten- or twentyfold. Only the rich could buy necessities, and even they could not use local money. Only with commodities like jewelry, gold coins, and American or Swiss currency could purchases be made. The poor faced starvation. They could barely get bread. Jews were worst off of all, since the Poles continued to point them out in the bread lines, getting them thrown out without even a crumb. The brutality blossomed in full view of the Poles, with their consent and cooperation.

The Roman Catholic Church was reluctant to help and, in some instances, advised churchgoers not to get involved in saving Jews. There were, of course, some who did not listen to the Church. A few Poles helped Jews in exchange for current valuables or future considerations.

The only newspaper officially available in Bedzin was the German daily *Der Sturmer,* which was edited by the famous Jew-hater Julius Streicher under the authority of the German propaganda ministry. With his editorials, Streicher incited the Polish populace to rise annd denounce the Jews. The paper's motto, which appeared each day above the date, announced: "The Jews are our misfortune."

Thus I learned what had developed while I struggled to get home. It was dawn when we finally paused for a few hours' sleep.

The People's Court

Life's new miseries continued to unfold, with a kaleidoscope of new horrors. We had no choice but to make the best of our circumstances.

When the invasion came, we could not imagine what was ahead for us. It was unbelievable that a nation of high culture should maim, kill, burn, destroy, uproot, and plan the extermination of a whole people. Nobody in his right mind could accept this as fact, or visualize Auschwitz, Dachau and the atrocities that were to come. Thus, no one intervened.

The myth of Jewish power was just a myth, as was the idea that all Jews were rich. The Jews proved unable to save themselves or to influence anybody else to save them. Jews outside Europe were occupied with their own problems.

In Poland, the Jews never had a leader of stature, despite numbering more than three million. In Bendin, the thirteen or more Jewish political parties could seldom agree on anything important.

We had been well prepared to endure suffering passively. In the Bible, it is written "an eye for an eye," but our elders had taught us to be glad we were left with one eye and could still see daylight.

My brothers and I were raised to turn from strife, never to resist or fight, even if we were attacked by Polish children or adults. I was forbidden even to carry a pocket knife; Papa said knives were for hooligans.

Still, as the days passed, I could see my papa, a believer,

who had always said, "It is God's will," begin to doubt. I had my own opinion.

Our town was incorporated into the German Reich, with its name changed to Bendsburg, o/s Upper Silesia.

I again worked for my uncle, whose shop was under direct German supervision and was only allowed to work for the German occupation force and for former civilian authorities who had taken over Jewish stores and apartments. The job provided me with a travel permit that allowed me to move relatively freely around the city, and prevented the Germans from grabbing me arbitrarily to do odd jobs.

Papa's butcher shop was also under supervision of a Treuhaender. It handled meat rations, which were supposed to be provided weekly but which were often missing when the distribution day came.

One Friday in October, 1939, Papa received 200 pounds of meat to be given out. About 2,000 people lined up outside the store, pushing and shoving each other. Mother, Papa, and Jack, who was fifteen at the time, divided the meat into weights appropriate for the ration cards. The pushing and shoving became so bad that they had to close the door and let in only five people at a time. This worked fine until some woman in the line started to yell: "The Jew is giving our rations away through the back door."

This was untrue—a back door didn't even exist—but that didn't stop her from smashing the glass front door with her fist. The ensuing commotion quickly attracted the German police.

A woman standing next to the woman who smashed the door got the Shupo's attention. "My name is Dryer, and I'm a Volksdeutsche," she said. She told them Jack smashed the woman's hand with a butcher knife and Papa had said, "Hitler's a big man now, but we'll cut him down to size."

The Shupo didn't need to hear anything more. Papa and Jack were escorted to the police station.

When I got home from work, everything was in disarray.

Mother was in tears. We had no word of what was to become of Papa and Jack, and no way to find out.

The next morning, Mother started contacting everyone we could think of who had connections with the Shupo, but nobody would touch the case.

We finally got word from a Pole who had been arrested and was at the station at the same time they were that they had been beaten into unconsciousness, brought to consciousness again by having buckets of urine thrown over them, and then beaten some more. This pattern was repeated again and again until Saturday morning. Then they were put into the city jail, and beaten again.

Since the charges against them were political, Papa and Jack came under the jurisdiction of the Gestapo, the Geheimestaatspolizei—secret state police. On Monday, two S.S. men came to the jail and took them to Gestapo headquarters in Katovic.

Everyone in town was talking about the incident. People looked at me with pity, as if I were already an orphan.

Mother, however, never gave up. From the first night, she began sleeping in her clothes, needing only to put on her shoes, should she have to get up quickly. As soon as she knew where they had been taken, she crossed into Germany, to Beuten, to consult Max "Israel" Boehm, the only Jewish attorney there legally admitted to represent Jewish prisoners. He accepted the case, but would give no indication that we had a chance to free them or even to ease their way. Still, he became Mother's only hope. At least we could prepare some kind of defense in case Papa came to trial. Mother crossed the border several times, without papers, disregarding the danger to herself to search out every avenue to help her husband and son.

At last, we got word that a Volksgericht (People's Court) would be held in November. We were told any competent witnesses we had would get permission to travel to Katovic for the hearing. We desperately sought witnesses, but everyone we talked to was afraid to testify, afraid even to travel to Katovic.

Finally, Mother found two people willing to take the chance and tell the truth. One was a veterinarian, a Pole and a major in the Polish army, and the second was a famous local soccer player named Bolek Cichon.

Mr. Boehm sent them travel permits for the court date, and Mother again crossed the border illegally, even though she couldn't be present in the room in the pre-war courthouse where the hearing was convened.

The court took note of our witnesses, who testified that neither of the women raising the charges had entered the store, that one had smashed the glass with her fist and that the other couldn't have talked to anyone inside because the door had been locked. The witnesses were dismissed, the court retired without handing down a decision, and we went back to waiting. Boehm wasn't even asked to speak.

Life went on, day in, day out. Mother still slept in her clothes, not giving up hope for a single moment.

The winter of 1939 was exceptionally cold. Our home was especially dark and gloomy with Papa and Jack gone. We didn't even know where they were being held, whether in prison or, perhaps, in a concentration camp. We did not know the results, if any, of the Volksgericht. Usually, these courts handed out death sentences left and right, without any right of appeal, but we heard nothing. If the Volksgericht could only hear our two witnesses, there would be a chance—one in a thousand—that some relief would be forthcoming.

When Papa and Jack were first incarcerated in the basement of Gestapo headquarters, another man from Bendin was with them. He had been a dealer in various goods before the invasion and was arrested for having a dozen cigarette lighters of the German "Thousand Cinders" brand in his home. No matter that he had sold these legally; possession of them had become a crime, especially for a Jew.

His wife and my mother, sharing hope and faith, became friends. They visited each other often, sharing their grief.

The other family included two sons and two daughters. The older son and daughter had left at the outset of the war for the east—Russia—and had not been heard from since. The younger son would eventually find his way into the forced labor camps. The younger daugher, Judy, was about my age, a very pretty girl with round black eyes; long, dark, shiny hair; and pearly white teeth. She was also very smart. We became friends, spending much time together, sharing our thoughts, our misfortune, and what enjoyment we could manage together.

One evening, in December of 1939, I was at her house. We talked and told stories, losing track of the time. Eventually we noticed that the clock showed eight, an hour past the curfew for Jews. How was I to get home? I became desperate. Panicky, I took off the white armband with its blue star of David, which I was required to wear to show I was a Jew, and ran like lightning. Poles could be out until ten. I could only hope I would pass. My heart beat rapidly as I moved like a shadow next to the buildings. It was about a mile to our house. My pulse raced. My footsteps were like thunder in my ears as I strained to hear any other sound. I reached the main street to our house. Two Shupo appeared, strolling along and talking, coming toward me from the direction of my home. My heart stopped. I had to make a quick decision. I couldn't go back because that would be very suspicious, so I lifted my head and went ahead. As I came even with the police, my legs became heavy, as if they were full of lead. They passed without any comment. I could breathe again. Within moments, I reached our building, which was locked exactly at seven by the live-in Polish janitor. I rang the bell perhaps three times before an angry voice asked who was there. I gave my name and was answered with a torrent of cursing in Polish. He called me everything from bastard to son-of-a-bitch to Christ-killer, but he let me in. I took his language in stride, being glad to be inside the big doors of the building. Without a word, I went up the stairs. It was not until I was safe in our apartment that I realized my stupidity. I should have slept in the corridor outside Judy's family's apartment, I thought. My run home could have cost me my life.

Daily, we continued to hope for a miracle. Mother crossed

the border periodically, risking her life to see the attorney in Beuten, but he couldn't do much. Then we got a letter saying a new hearing was scheduled for February of 1940, this time at Gestapo headquarters. At least we knew Papa and Jack were still jailed nearby.

Mother went for the hearing and waited outside the room, praying for a favorable outcome. All she could do was talk to Boehm, who also knew nothing. He was permitted inside but, again, was not asked to speak, and, again, we were not told of any decision being reached.

More weeks went by. Then, one evening in early March of 1940, we heard footsteps on the stairs. It was after nine, past curfew, but the footfall sounded like Papa's. There was a knock on the door. I opened it, and, to our grateful surprise, Papa walked in, followed by Jack. We looked but were at first unable to believe our eyes. Mother burst into tears. It was a miracle: two Jews, accused of insulting Hitler and put in the hands of the Gestapo, freed from jail and issued passes to travel home.

All the neighbors gathered and made blessings over Papa and Jack as if they had come back from the dead. It was the talk of all Bendin.

A short time later, Judy's father was also released, on the strength of bribes placed by her family with influential officials. He had no work to go back to and eventually disappeared into the concentration camps.

We recuperated from our ordeal and tried to lead as normal a life as possible. Passover came. We didn't realize this was to be the last Passover our whole family would share. Mother was in an especially good mood, having gotten Papa and Jack back safely. Their presence gave deeper meaning to our celebration of the Festival of Freedom, and yet we were still the slaves of our era, in greater jeopardy than the Israelites under Pharaoh before Moses led them from bondage. We didn't have a Moses to free us. Our brethren in the West were silent. We didn't have even an ordinary leader to guide us, to teach us, to comfort us. We were like sheep without a shepherd. The lightness of previous Passovers was missing; we were bracing ourselves for the unknown.

In the meantime, Germany brought the Blitzkrieg to its western front. Little happened in the war until May of 1940 when the Germans invaded Belgium, Holland, Luxembourg, and France. Another hope of mankind was being extinguished.

The German Army marched into Paris after six weeks of fighting. Hitler came to Paris for the signing of France's surrender. Britain now stood alone against the victorious German army, rallying behind Sir Winston Churchill, who promised:

> We will fight on the beaches;
> we will defend our island whatever the cost may be;
> we will fight in the streets;
> we will fight in the fields and hills;
> we shall never surrender.

The English never deviated from this declaration. They fought in the skies above them, with the victory of their Spitfires over the Luftwaffe giving hope to all the oppressed people in Europe. The British faced every hardship, standing alone against Hitler's Reich. A hundred thousand people died in the bombing of Britain.

London became a home for Europe's hopes for freedom, literally as well as figuratively. Czech, Polish, Norwegian, Dutch, and French exiles, who refused to surrender, based themselves there, directing the undergrounds that brought hope to their captive countrymen. Theirs was an unconquerable spirit opposing the German hordes and what they stood for, but the defeat of tyranny was a long way off.

Hitler and the Nazis, drunk with their victories in the west, quietly prepared to attack the east. Though the invasion of Russia in 1941 would come as a shock to the world, it was not a surprise to us. As I stood on the main street of Bendin in July, 1940, German tanks, artillery, and troops passed by, headed east. On each vehicle was written, *"Von Frankreich durch Polen gehen wir die Russian holen"* (we're going from France through Poland to get the Russians).

Germany seemed invincible. All of western Europe, except

Switzerland and Sweden, were under Hitler's control. Hungary, Romania, and Bulgaria became his allies.

Then on the eve of Yom Kippur, the Day of Atonement, I was requested to come for my medical examination before going to Germany and slave labor. I felt as though I were locked in a cage, with only a dark future ahead.

Forced labor in our town (1939)

Polish police and S.S. men making fun of a Jew (1939)

PART II: THE CAMPS

R.A.B. Lager Klein Mangersdorf

The train came to an abrupt halt. I woke up sweating. Outside it was cold, rainy and growing dark. It was 5:00 P.M.

All hell broke loose. The S.A. men ran up and down the platform yelling "*Alle raus. Schnell. Antreten*" (everyone out. Quick. Quick. Fall in).

I took my plywood suitcase, and out I went. From the platform, I could read the name of the station: Krappitz. I had no idea where Krappitz was, but I knew I was in the lion's den. About 100 of the group from Bendin got off with the rest continuing to other camps.

Yelling, pushing and shoving continued for about ten minutes until everybody was in line at attention. We learned the German military language quickly to avoid being hit with what the S.A. called an Ochsenzimmer, a dried bull's penis, which felt like a piece of lead pipe. We were formed into four lines and counted like sheep. A top S.A. man named Lulu took our guards' report with a Nazi salute: "All one hundred Jews present." Then came the order "Upmarschieren" (forward march).

Off we went in the rain, each of us carrying his belongings and his fears of the unknown. We didn't expect a holiday, and we knew we were there to work. Work, we did not fear, but we didn't know what our living conditions would be, except that they were likely to be bad. We had seen what the S.A. was capable of in town and could imagine what they would do in a camp where they had full control.

None of us knew how far we had to march. Within about

fifteen minutes, we were crossing farmland. It must have rained all day, or longer, and the fields were mud that sucked at our boots and shoes, catching them so we could only go on by pulling our feet out of them and continuing unshod. The march, though just begun, had already become an ordeal.

Anyone who fell behind the columns was hit and forced to catch up and retake his place. Some of the marchers threw away their luggage, which they would need so badly later.

After about ninety minutes, we reached our new home. The newly built wooden barracks were on three sides of a large dirt quadrangle. They were of prefabricated construction with raised floors, designed so they could be moved as our work site changed. Each included a series of rooms, which, we were to discover, contained ten double bunks. The one closest to the gate through the barbed-wire fence that surrounded the whole area included the camp office, kitchen, and dining room, as well as two sleeping rooms, and the one across from it held a medical office and six rooms. The third long barrack had seven sleeping rooms. Along the fourth side of the quadrangle was the wash barrack, with its laundry and showers, and the outhouse. At each corner of the fence was a guardhouse, built to give the S.A. guards a birdseye view of the whole area. The troopers lived in a separate barrack outside the fence in the corner near the gate.

We were marched into the compound past a sign which read "Reichs Autobahn Lager III Klein Mangersdorf" (German highway camp Klein Mangersdorf III). We joined Jews from other towns near Bendin, who had arrived in the camp two or three days before we had. The group included Mr. Ziban from Sosnowitz, the Jewish elder for the camp. He had been appointed to be in charge of all the Jews in Mangersdorf before we were drafted. All the preparations were made by the Jewish Boards of Elders in our home towns. Before Germany invaded Poland, we had elected the boards to handle matters of community interest. Afterwards, the elected leaders were replaced by appointees who would work with the conquerors.

Inside the yard, we were again ordered to stand at attention in columns. *"Muetzen auf,"* came the order, followed once again, by a count, this time of the entire camp, about 250 people. Then came the report to the commandant, accompanied by a Nazi salute: "All Jews present. Heil Hitler."

"Ruehrt euch" (at ease), we were ordered, and then we were told to assemble in the mess hall. The buildings were too new to have electricity or water yet, and there were no tables or chairs. We sat on the floor. The guards had some of the newly arrived prisoners bring in three big containers of rice and ordered us each to pick up a bowl and spoon and line up to get our portions. Response to the order was mixed, with many of us too exhausted to eat and others refusing for religious reasons.

The civilian commandant of the camp, whose name was Kramer and who looked nine months pregnant, was furious that the order was not immediately and uniformly obeyed.

"From now on, you'll get only water, bread, and kohlrabi soup," he screamed. He kept his word for about four weeks, to teach the "Jewish pigs" a lesson.

At last, we were assigned to rooms. Each of us was given a bunk with a straw-filled sack for a mattress; a pillow, also filled with straw; and a blanket. I climbed into my upper bunk, removed my wet clothes, and soon fell into a deep sleep.

The next morning, a Monday, we were awakened at 5:00 A.M., given bread and an ersatz coffee made from grain, and marched into the yard. There, everyone in camp was put into colonies or work groups of fifty and assigned a *"Kolonie Fuehrer"* (group leader). Group leaders were picked by Mr. Ziban, who made additional assignments as we stood at attention. Three men were ordered to work in the kitchen and two to finish the plumbing in the wash barrack. Willy, a furrier who had come to Bendin in 1938 with the Jews fleeing Germany after the Kristallnacht, was named "Sanitater" (medic). These, and later appointments, which were made as they were needed, generally went to those who spoke fluent German and were more mature and respected by their fellows.

The organizational work finished, we workers marched, in

groups, through the gate for our first day's work. It took about fifteen minutes to reach the *"Baustelle"* (construction site). There, we were each given a shovel and a pick and put to work leveling the right-of-way for a highway. Our job was to move hills to fill ditches. We were paired off along a temporary narrow-gauge rail line that ran from the hills to the ditches. A train of forty to fifty cars stood on the track, and two of us were assigned to each car. The guards told us we had to dig ten cubic yards of earth each hour to fill our car. The train was pulled by a steam engine fired by wood and coal and driven by a German. The guards told us the engineer didn't like to be late. "Every hour, on the hour, the train leaves." they said, "and your cars had better be full." Each time a loaded train pulled out, a set of empty cars was pulled in so we could continue our labors. We discovered that, if we finished before the hour was up, we could get a little rest until the next cars arrived.

Our supervisor was a Pole named Wojtyla. The only German words he knew were "Schnell. Schnell. Bewegt Euch, Ihre verfluchte Hunde" (Quick. Quick. Shake it up, you cursed dogs). For the next eight months, we heard Wojtyla repeat the same words over and over for twelve hours each day, except Sunday. He was always picking up tree branches to carry, and many times each day he broke one over somebody's head or back. Wojtyla was especially vicious on Friday evenings and Saturdays, the Jewish sabbath.

Though occasionally one of the guards would announce his name to us, we were never introduced to most of them, so we christened them with our own nicknames. Lulu, the S.A. commandant, with his red face, swollen, heavily veined nose, and beerbelly hanging over his belt, we called "the Drunk." There was "Freckle Face"; "Cotton Ass," whose pants hung virtually unfilled in back; "Hole Face," whose complexion had apparently suffered from a childhood bout with chickenpox; and "Red Cheeks," who was always yelling, with or without provocation. Another character, who did introduce himself, warning us to mark him well and "beware of crossing Arthur Lux," had a Hitler-style mustache and was vicious to Jews, unless they were women.

Day in and day out, without adequate food, we did twelve hours of heavy work. We started figuring how long we could survive on those rations, but it was a hollow exercise, since we had no one to complain to.

On Sundays, we washed our clothes, cleaned shoes, mended socks, scrubbed barracks, and emptied the manure from the outhouse, filling containers which farmers from the surrounding area picked up to use on their fields. Sometimes, we wished Mondays came sooner.

After several days of digging, our work site was moved to the edge of a swampy pond that was to be filled in for the Autobahn. Though the right-of-way was not prepared all the way to the new site, the bosses wanted us to get some of the watery work done before the pond froze.

The rails were laid parallel to the edge of the pond, and we were issued rubber boots and ordered by Wojtyla to clear the *"Mutter Boden,"* the black dirt from the bottom of the pond. This rich muck was sent to farmers and replaced with a more solid landfill, which would support the highway.

So into the water we went, sinking well beyond the depth of our boots. Each evening, we dried our socks and pants, only to have them soaked through again the first thing the next day.

We dug out the mud, loaded it into the cars, and replaced it with rock, sand, and gravel. Then we would move the rails to keep them by the water's edge. Moving the rails was especially hard, with the men wading through water to shift them and sometimes falling under the weight full length in the chilly liquid. We dredged the swamp until late November, 1940, when frost set in and it became unworkable.

We were glad to be back at our first work site, filling car after car, train after train, with dry dirt and moving rail sections on our backs.

After our return, I acquired a new chore. Cotton Ass, each morning at eleven forty-five, just before lunch break, had me dig a hole in the woods near the site. I was quickly chased off when the task was done. We wondered what was going on until we spotted him walking through the trees with his girl friend, a woman from a nearby town who had a hunchback.

About one month after arriving at the camp, we were given permission to write home. We were each given one postcard and told to write only in German. The cards would be censored by the S.A., we were warned, and no nonsense would be tolerated.

Despite the precautions, somehow a message got through to our homes about our desperate lack of food and necessities. Packages started to arrive. All food was confiscated, but such things as toothbrushes, toothpaste, shoe polish, shirts, and jackets were delivered. My parents sent me a hat in which they had hidden fifty marks. In the note with the package they wrote, "Regards from Uncle Mutze." *Mutze* means cap, and, since I had no uncle by that name, I took it as a clue to examine closely the hat they had sent me. The money was hidden between the cardboard pieces that stiffened the small bill of the soft cap. As word of the ruse got around camp, it became common for everyone to write home asking to be sent "Harry's chapeau"—money. At other times, regards from Uncle Vest or Uncle Coat would pinpoint funds from home.

The money was useful in obtaining necessities in the black market that developed in the camp. At first, such staples as tobacco, sewing supplies, and mirrors could be purchased in a canteen located near the kitchen. However, about three months after we opened the camp, the canteen ran out of merchandise. It closed and never reopened.

Christmas came, bringing my first birthday in a German camp. We received special rations for the holiday—some sausage, marmalade, and a thicker soup than usual. The guards got drunk and jolly and wanted to be entertained, so they gathered us to put on a spontaneous camp show. Everyone who could sing, improvise music, or play an instrument participated.

Shortly after Christmas, winter set in with a vengeance, making work on the Autobahn impossible. Since we weren't working, our already meager rations were cut in half. We received half a pound of bread, kohlrabi soup, a piece of margarine and ersatz coffee. We got our first taste of being hungry day in and day out. The only break in routine came after each snow, when we were sent to clean up nearby towns and villages. We prayed for winter to end quickly so we could go back to the road work—and the full measure of our starvation diets.

When we did return to the Autobahn, at the beginning of March, 1941, I was promoted to assistant *"Lok Fuehrer,"* helping run a locomotive on the narrow rails. The elder had asked for someone mechanically inclined for the job, and I had volunteered, so there I was, fueling and oiling the engine, connecting cars, and praying that nothing would go wrong.

After we'd been in the camp for three months, we wrote home to ask if we would be relieved. The answer was not heartening. More and more Jews were being taken for forced labor; there was no one to relieve us.

As often as we were permitted to get mail, I would receive postcards from home and from Judith. They were written with tears and love, and I cherished them.

Judith, a frequent visitor at my parents' house, asked if she could join the camp. By then, the Germans had a few women in each camp for office, kitchen, and laundry duties. Our hardships were not for her, I felt, and managed to advise her through my parents against volunteering. Months later, I regretted this advice. In 1943, she was shipped to Auschwitz and shared the destiny of the Jews of that time. Perhaps she might have had a better chance to survive had she been in the labor camps, I thought later, when I learned her fate.

Our work was hard. Quite a few of the men suffered hernias and were sent home for surgery. From them, our parents learned the truth about how we were being treated.

I had only one prayer at that time: to get rid of Wojtyla. He was worse than the Germans, with his nonstop cursing and his constant swinging of often-broken tree branches. He left several of my fellow inmates crippled.

Our guards were shifted among the "colonies," but we got to know them a little. The Germans admired me for my hard work and occasionally singled me out with other hard workers for an extra food ration—perhaps an additional bowl of soup. I watched my pace, however, particularly after it pushed some of my co-workers too hard, and they asked me to slow down.

One day, during the lunch break, Freckle Face started a conversation with me. He took a kind of liking to me, and we began to chat somewhat regularly. He told me he was from Koenigs Huette, a big industrial town on the German-Polish border. His father was German and his mother Polish, and he had joined the S.A. secretly in 1936 in Poland. All Germans had to join the military, and he had volunteered to avoid conscription and to garner the privileges that came with joining freely.

Still, he told me, he hated war and everthing connected with it. The S.A. didn't have an easy life either. The guards got only three days' furlough a month, the pay was poor, and they had to buy their own uniforms.

I told him that I was a journeyman plumber and my father had a butcher shop in Bendsburg, only eighteen kilometers from his hometown. Eventually, I suggested that if, on his next furlough, he were to visit my parents, they would give him enough money to cover his train fare and schnapps, plus a little extra. He said he'd think about it and let me know.

A few days later, Freckle Face came over to where I was working, took me aside, and said he would visit. "I'm going home next Friday for three days," he said. "Prepare a letter to your parents, and, when I get back, I'll give you an answer from them so you'll know I was there."

I wrote a long letter in Jewish, describing for the first time what had transpired since I left home. I didn't give every gruesome detail because I wanted to save my parents some grief.

The next day, I gave the letter and my parents' address to my new friend, with my fingers crossed all the while, thinking that if that letter fell into the wrong hands or if he changed his mind I was done for. I'd become a statistic.

For the next four days, dreams troubled me: A man in the yellow uniform of the S.A. knocking on my parents' door—their hearts might stop from fear. Ah, well, what was done was done.

Everything was in motion, and all I could do was wait for Freckle Face to return.

Many months later, I learned that fear had indeed followed him to my parents'. When they saw him coming, all the neighbors had ducked out of sight. Jack answered the door, Freckle Face introduced himself (though by role, not name) and thereafter everyone's fear was replaced by curiosity about his presence. My grateful family covered his expenses as promised.

It was a Thursday when I finally saw Freckle Face again, taking out another colony of Jews. I couldn't talk with him, but, from his face, I could read that the mission had been accomplished.

It wasn't until Saturday that he was assigned to our colony. The hours of anticipation had become unbearable. Saturday morning was the worst. Finally, at lunch time, he signaled me to follow him. He gave me a four-page letter in Yiddish from Papa, a letter in German from my brother Jack, pictures from my parents' brothers and Judith, 100 German marks and some canned meat and fat. I was in heaven. I couldn't risk reading the letters then, but I thanked him and said I hoped we would be similarly in touch again. I couldn't wait until we finished work. I didn't wash, nor did I stay in line for soup that day. I went to my bed and read the letters—perhaps fifty times each—and looked at the pictures and cried. I was a little less lonesome. At least I had made contact with the outside world, though I couldn't reveal this to anyone, even to my closest friend, because it might endanger Freckle Face. I was like a newly born soul; I could move mountains. What a difference a few quickly written words and some pictures could make for me.

Though I was thrilled by having contact with home, the news was not comforting. Rumor had it that all Jews were to be moved to a ghetto. Rations had been cut to a bare minimum. People were selling their clothes to the Poles for a decent meal. Rich and poor were in the same boat, and people shared whatever they had. Thanks to a decent *Treuhander*—a butcher from Germany who supervised several shops—Papa's shop still got meat and canned pork to fill ration cards. My family would not starve, but no one knew how long those circumstances would last. At least life in camp was routine—work, sleep, work, sleep, work, and more work—and without the uncertainties of home. I couldn't wait until Freckle Face got his next furlough so I could, perhaps, get more first-hand information on what was happening there.

Work and sleep—life in camp went on. We had a lot of injuries, and every few weeks, as they were needed, transports carried the sick or injured to the *Durchganglager* (transit camp) in Sosnowitz, six kilometers from Bendin. They were checked by German doctors, repaired as well as possible, and either sent back to camp or freed and sent home. The trains that took them away returned equal numbers of personnel—either those who had recovered or their replacements.

Willy, our medic, cured all sickness with aspirin. He was empowered to keep the ailing in sick bay for a day or so, but he never did. Once I had to go to him because I had a terrible toothache. Willy just smiled goodnaturedly, took a pair of ordinary pliers, and pulled out my tooth. The whole inside of my mouth became infected. I couldn't eat for three days. But miracles do happen, and this time, with Willy's aspirins, I recovered.

In the middle of April, 1940, Freckle Face told me to prepare another letter. He would get his monthly furlough the next week and would be glad to visit my family again. I asked him if he could possibly visit them in civilian clothes so they and the neighbors wouldn't be shaken up by his uniform. He said that was impossible.

"In this uniform," he said, "I have freedom to move without being disturbed by anybody."

I acquiesced because I had no other choice; this link meant so much to me. It was a pity I couldn't share it with my fellow inmates.

As I wrote and waited, one of our group leaders escaped, a man named Jacob. He had been guarded loosely because he was a colony leader. I later found out that he obtained papers as an S.A. man and lived through the war as such. His escape made things harder for us. Stricter guards, with German shepherds at their sides, were brought in. All official correspondence with home was cut off. All arriving packages were confiscated. The guards became less friendly. There was talk that they would be mobilized and sent to a new eastern front. It was all rumors, but we conducted our own war based on them, discussing strategy and extrapolating events. Some of us proved excellent strategists, and I believe that if Herr Hitler had had a few of them, he would never have lost the war.

My waiting for Freckle Face's return became a counting of days, hours, minutes, seconds. The day I saw him lined up again for duty, my whole spirit lifted. I counted the seconds until I could reach out for the few words my papa had written in Yiddish. It was memorable. I had never realized what a letter could mean, how your insides could tremble in anticipation of hiding to read and reread and read again those words, devouring them over and over—and then lying down and dreaming of a different world, of being free again, without watchdogs and barbed wire and guards. Sometimes I wished I could be a bird and fly wherever my heart desired, but this freedom was not to be for a long time. I had been in camp six months. Though I didn't know it then, four more long years were to follow.

The day of his return, Freckle Face was assigned to guard our group. A movement of his eyes showed he was searching for me. The opportunity to talk came, again, at lunch break. He called me aside and handed me a letter and a small package containing new pajamas, a couple of shirts, and underwear. The clothes were timely, but the letter was crucial. I took it and opened it. I began to read; I just couldn't wait until evening. The letter described life in Bendin, which was becoming more difficult each day. It was full of love and advice, compassion and sorrow; it was full of tears, even to teardrops on the paper, full of hope and strength. My family's immediate worry was Jack, who was going on seventeen and next in line to be drafted into forced labor.

I hid my treasure away from everyone and decided that, in May, when Freckle Face had his next furlough, I would write in more detail about life in camp, mostly to tell Jack what to expect.

Work on our section of the Autobahn was in its final stages. I had been moved to the colony doing fine grading of the road, and time passed uneventfully. We tamped and smoothed using shovels and muscle.

May came, and I wrote an eight-page letter describing life in camp. I told Jack what necessities to bring to get by on a day-to-day basis. That was how we had to live, hoping only to survive to the next dawn, though sustained by hope of a better someday. We couldn't, or shouldn't, think about tomorrow, for tomorrow never existed, I wrote. Impatiently, I waited for Freckle Face's next monthly furlough.

At long last, his furlough came. When Freckle Face returned, he brought two letters, one from my parents and one, in Polish, from Judith. He also brough two sweaters which Judith had knit for me. These, I cherished.

Work on our section of the highway was nearing completion, but was still not done when, on June 22, without warning, the workers were kept in camp instead of being marched off to the job. We didn't know why we weren't working in the middle of the week, but it was obvious something was going to change. In the midst of our confusion, we were ordered to pack and be ready to leave. We were being transferred to other camps.

As I moved to obey, I was in shock. I couldn't believe that my contact with home was going to be broken. I prepared myself for the worst, as I gathered my battered, padlocked plywood suitcase.

As we prepared, there was commotion all around. Rumors flew, from which we realized that existing nonaggression pacts had been violated and Germany had finally added the Soviet Union to the list of countries it was fighting. I heard the news from Freckle Face. He told me the guards, too, were expecting marching orders.

Hitler's invasion of the U.S.S.R. on June 22 provided World War II with an aspect of unlimited barbarism. All that had already happened—the destruction of Poland and Western Europe and the Balkans and the bombing of Great Britain—paled beside the loss of life and the destruction that began with that act. Blitzkrieg was to reach a scale beyond comprehension on the vast Russian lands.

Though the invasion did not surprise those of us who had watched the troops moving through Bedzin a year before, to the rest of the world it was a shock. The massive thrust came along a front 3,000 miles long, from Leningrad to Smolensk. The Russian army caved in before it. During the first week of fighting, hundreds of thousands of men were taken prisoners, some of whom we were to see first hand at our next camps. In the first year of fighting in the East, the Soviet Union would lose four to five million men, and there would remain three more years of war.

At about 3:00 P.M., six big military trucks pulled up to the gates. They were driven and guarded by Shutzpolizei. Our new camps were under Shupo supervision. I didn't regret leaving a place where we had left so much sweat and tears, but we had to brace ourselves, once more, for the unknown.

As the fighting began to the east, we were summoned for roll call. We had to fall into line—we had become really good at that—as uncertainty hung in the air. We were sorted into lots of fifty, counted and recounted, and loaded into the trucks, which left in different directions. We waved goodbye to our comrades, to some for the last time.

R.A.B. Lager Rogau

Our truck, with its fifty laborers, headed for a transit camp named Rogau. The other five trucks went elsewhere. The ride took about three hours. Our leader was Baruch Gaftek, who later fought in the Bendin ghetto uprising. Our guards were Shutzpolizei, who were older than the S.A. guards and didn't look as vicious.

Rogau was set up similarly to Klein Mangersdorf, with prefabricated wood barracks around an open field and barbed wire around everything. When we arrived, we were dispersed to various barracks, where we waited for the veteran inmates to return from work so we could find out what awaited us in this new paradise.

At 6:00 P.M., the gates opened, and the oldtimers marched into the compound. They were put through the customary routine: "Halt." *"Muetzen auf."* Counted. "Sixty Jews reporting back. All present." The Nazi salute.

They were dismissed, and we came up to greet our new comrades in suffering. They were from different parts of Poland and, at first, looked on us newcomers with suspicion. However, after a few hours, the common elements of suffering, survival, and Jewishness surfaced, and the ice was broken.

As we talked, we found that, thus far, Rogau had been easier to live in than Mangersdorf. The rations were larger than ours had been, and the work was easier. The mail policy was more lax: you could write postcards twice a month and receive two postcards from home. The Shupo were more lenient and more kindly in their treatment of the workers than the S.A.

We lined up for rations, telling and retelling our new friends our experiences of the last eight months.

The next morning, the guards woke us at 5:00 A.M. We washed, formed a line for coffee—or what passed for coffee—and at 5:30 colonies, as usual, were formed. Off we marched to our construction site, called Sakrau, which was along the same Autobahn route as our Mangersdorf site. Our job was to pour concrete for a bridge over the Autobahn. We were divided into work groups of six. My group unloaded cement bags from a railroad car and brought them to the cement mixer in an uninterrupted stream.

At Sakrau, I saw my cousin Serge, who had been an architecture student before the war. We embraced; I was thrilled to see someone close. He was a colony leader, and I was able to get permission to leave the work line for an hour and talk with him. We talked about our family and the past months. He promised to write home about me, and, in fact, a week later I got a food package from my aunt, Serge's mother. I hoped we would be in that camp long enough to enjoy each other's company, but this was a transit camp, and I knew my stay was temporary.

When we were not working, we had free movement within the confines of the camp. I explored what there was to explore, chatting with the workers who handled the daily functions of existence. I made friends with the camp's office girl, Gerda, who was from Katovic. With her help, I managed to take special mail privileges and send a postcard each week. I also managed to get assigned to Serge's colony. I became custodian of the tools, oiling and repairing them and generally keeping them in shape. It was a relatively easy job, and one I knew.

But these good things didn't last long. After only two months, and without warning, many of my comrades from Mangersdorf and I were ordered to pack and be ready to leave. The guards went through camp as we dressed, singling out those to go until they had fifty Jews for shipping. Panic struck us again. We began to speculate on where destiny would bring us next. When our co-workers marched out to their daily labors, we were left behind. I couldn't even say goodbye to Serge.

About midday, a truck arrived for us. For some unknown reason, Baruch remained behind. The underground eventually got him home, where he became a prominent Zionist leader. For the rest of us, there was again the routine: we were lined up, counted, loaded, and shipped away.

Z.A.L. Annaberg

Shortly before nightfall, we arrived at the gates of Zwangarbeits Lager Annaberg, a forced-labor camp. From the outside it looked much like our previous two camps, with its full complement of prefabs, but including some permanent structures that had been there for years and were being used to house workers since the camp was very crowded.

We were ordered to get off the truck and assemble in an old theater with flea-infested straw on the floor. We were tired, but we couldn't sleep; the fleas ate us alive.

Annaberg contained Jews from Auschwitz and Chzanow, in Galicia, which was an Austrian territory before World War I. They referred to us as "the Polish Jews," and there was friction between our groups. We newcomers got the dirtiest and most difficult work.

As we settled into a new camp, it was usual to ask around to see if there was anyone already there who we knew. Who's here from my hometown, we would ask. In Annaberg, my questioning was rewarded with news that an old school friend of mine named Israel was there. We had shared a two-seater bench in sixth and seventh grades.

Accordingly, I kept my eyes open and was rewarded after a couple of days. I hailed him, and we embraced, exclaiming our pleasure at being together and exchanging the stories of how we had reached Annaberg.

Israel and three other men from Bendin were with the Galicians because they had been on a kibbutz outside of Auschwitz preparing to emigrate to Palestine as chalutz—pioneers—when the Jews in that area were rounded up. All four were in Annaberg.

I told Israel of our plight in the theater, and how the fleas made it impossible to sleep and get enough rest so we could manage the heavy work we were assigned. He said he would do something, but only for me.

Sure enough, at nightfall, after our soup, I was called and told I could move in with Israel and share his berth. Compared with the theater floor, it was a paradise. I also got to go to the construction site with the oldtimers and avoid the abuse we "Polish Jews" had been receiving.

Israel was well respected by his fellows. He behaved well and had developed personal pull with the elders. Thus, he was able to arrange the unofficial favor of moving me to his berth, which we shared as long as I was in Annaberg. I wasn't supposed to be there, but our roommates covered for us and the guards didn't generally keep track of individuals. That was up to the colony leaders. The Jewish administration of the camp decided who went where.

The Germans did keep excellent and precise records, since laborers were hired for jobs, and individuals and agencies had to be carefully billed. Their concern, however, was with how many Jews were on a job—we were counted and recounted as we entered and left for assignments—not which ones.

At Annaberg, we met Russian prisoners-of-war for the first time. They, too, were used as laborers. The main assignments for all of us were at another point along the same Autobahn we had worked on at Klein Mangersdorf and Rogau.

We only saw them at a distance on the work site, however, since they were imprisoned in another camp, in the woods some distance from us. Their situation was critical. They looked like *mussulmen*—walking skeletons, on their last legs. From the rare occasions when a Jew managed to talk with a Russian, we learned that they had been captured on the first German thrust into the Soviet Union. They told us all political commissars and, especially, Jewish prisoners-of-war, had been shot in cold blood. The rest had been consigned to forced labor.

As meager as our daily rations were—200 grams of bread, some hot soup, a little marmalade and margarine and the ersatz coffee—theirs were less, only half as much bread and hot water. Hunger clawed at their humanity, reducing them to less than beasts. When one of them died, the others cut pieces from the corpse and ate. It made me ill whenever someone died at work, and I saw this happen.

We decided that we had to help somehow and decided that half our meager lunchtime rations should be given to the POWs. Our colony organized to leave food behind at the site where they would find it. We started this shortly after we arrived at Annaberg and continued doing it until we left. We had to act in strict secrecy, since to be discovered passing food by the S.S. men guarding them or the Shupo guarding us would have meant being hanged. Fortunately, no one was caught.

After about three months at Annaberg, there came again a day when we were kept in camp. It was apparent that we were again to be moved. We hoped for the best, but we were not optimistic. As the battle on the eastern front had lengthened, our treatment had worsened. Thousands of Russians were surrendering or being caught. They were shipped to our area, crowding the camps and leading the Germans to disperse the Jews to other areas to make room. The best I could realistically hope for was to go in the same group as Israel.

By midmorning, trucks arrived to pick us up. We were counted into groups, and, luckily, Israel and I were together, along with the other men of his group from the kibbutz. The Shutzpolizei loaded us, with count and salute, and off we drove.

Z.A.L. Ottmuth

Late in the afternoon, we arrived at Zwangarbeits Lager Ottmuth, on the Oder River. We were greeted by the Jewish elder, a nice-looking man from Czechoslovakia named Haubenstock. To our surprise, we found ourselves in the care of S.A. men from Mangersdorf. Unluckily for me, Freckle Face was not among them. I later found out that he was sent to the Russian front. But there were Arthur Lux, still wearing Hitler's mustache; Cotton Ass; and Red Cheeks. Those of us who had been at Mangersdorf were recognized and separated out for special treatment. I managed to bring Israel and his companions from the kibbutz with us. Lux told the elder we were the best group of workers and would show the others how the work was to be done. We, and especially I, breathed a sigh of relief on hearing such words from the S.A.

We were assigned rooms and berths, once more in divided prefabricated wooden barracks. I took a bunk below Israel, and we promised to share our lot, no matter what.

The next day we were assigned to load coal into boats on the Oder. We carried baskets weighing 100 pounds onto the boat, walking the twenty feet from shore to deck on parallel six-inch–wide planks. With empty baskets, we left the boat by another pair of boards. Occasionally, someone would fall off and either swam to the boat or was thrown ropes. No one drowned during the two weeks we were on that job. Next, we were assigned to bridge-building duty, a strenuous job that left us constantly looking forward to Sunday, the rest day. Unfortunately, after six days of work, most of us were drafted for Sunday work, too: such tasks as cleaning out the outhouses, washing the barracks' floors, washing windows, and cleaning the grounds.

On the construction site, we had a *Polier* (superintendent) who wore a big Nazi medal. He pushed us to the extreme and, at every excuse for an excuse, hit us with a stick.

As we moved from camp to camp, we were able to notify our families of where to write, so we still received postcards from home. There, conditions had also become progressively worse. Many of my contemporaries had been drafted and sent to forced labor camps. Mother had volunteered to work for a German shop that made uniforms, mostly for the Wehrmacht. Working for the "Rosner Shop" also protected her from being transported. Papa, Jack, and Sam were safe for the time being, since Papa worked in his shop for the *Treuhander* and Jack worked for that "German" concern. Sam, who was twelve, was being educated at home by a special tutor. Their employment gave my family passes to move around Bendsburg, except where the Germans lived. Without the passes, they would have been stuck within prescribed Jewish areas of the city. From time to time, I received packages from home, which I shared with Israel. They were a welcome sign of life.

Work on the bridge continued. My assignment changed from day to day. I unloaded cement, shoveled dirt, mixed concrete, cleaned tools, poured cement. Like everyone else, I had good days and bad days. At the end of November for a couple of weeks, I was given the relatively easy assignment of driving the diesel machine that delivered cement and removed piles of dirt from the site.

In the meantime, an apparently mellowed Lux became my best friend. I guessed he knew about my arrangement with Freckle Face and later found out they had shared the vodka Freckle Face received from Jack when he delivered my letters to my home.

Occasionally, when Lux had duty inside the camp in the evenings, he called on me to keep him company. At first, I was afraid, but slowly I got used to this. He had me tell him the story of my life, the story of the Jews in pre-war Poland, and of our life in general. His attitudes had been altered by a Jewish woman, and he was curious to learn more about us than he had found out from the anti-Semitic ravings of Julius Streicher and his newspaper, *Der Sturmer*. He had never had any contact with Jews before drawing guard duty in the camps. He had found us to be able workers, doing whatever we were assigned competently and without complaint. He found us to be educated and quick to learn whatever we needed to know. I explained to him that learning, to us, was a matter of life and death, a matter of survival.

We talked about religion, politics, and, naturally, the war. Lux told me that, with the German army having captured half of Russia, the war would end soon and I would go home to my own trade.

Early in our relationship, Lux told me that whenever I needed something and he could help, I should ask him. Such an occasion soon arose. A package came from home. In it, there were supposed to be, among other things, two cans of meat. I am sure my family had saved it by not eating so I could have some extra food. The two cans were gone. I figured it was the time to test Lux.

I managed to contact him and tell him about the missing cans. About fifteen minutes later, the Jewish elder appeared in my room with the two cans. He said they had fallen out of the cardboard box and he hadn't known to whom they belonged. Naturally, that was cockamamie bullshit. Also naturally, I later found I had invited trouble for myself by putting the "King of the Jews" of Ottmuth on the spot. I had to watch myself from then on, and always stay on my toes.

Haubenstock was a nice fellow until he was crossed. He ruled his kingdom with rigor and discipline and would neither tolerate nor forget a challenge. He had a spy network among the inmates, which reported every unusual thing that occurred each day at each construction site. At times, I wished I hadn't talked to Lux, but what was done couldn't be undone.

At mid-December, 1941, the bridge work had to be stopped because of cold weather. We were moved indoors, assigned to work at a paper mill, unloading coal from trains and loading it into furnaces, loading massive rolls of paper onto trains, cleaning up debris, and oiling the machines.

I was at first assigned to various jobs, but soon they asked anyone who was a mechanic to come forward. Normally, I didn't volunteer, not wanting to become prominent. Lying low, I felt, gave me a better chance to survive. Besides, I wasn't up to being in authority. Who was I to punish others? In this case, however, I stepped forward and announced my skill.

As a mechanic, I was assigned to care for the factory machinery. This kept me inside, where it was warm, instead of outside in the bitter cold and snow.

One day, a goodlooking girl who worked on a paper-bag assembly line that I was often near told me to look under one of the machines. Women made up most of the labor force of the factory, and I had talked briefly with this woman before. She was German, and every German had the authority to order around any Jew, so I did as I was told. In a corner on the floor, I found a couple of liverwurst sandwiches, wrapped in newspaper, which she indicated I should take. I had them until we assembled to go back to camp. The next day, I was again ordered under the machine, and again I found sandwiches.

This routine continued for about five days. Then, I found a note with the food. The girl wrote that her name was Gertrude, and she was from near Katovic. She wrote that she was willing to help me escape and to hide me as long as the war lasted. The thought of escape shook me, bringing thousands of plans to my mind. I could hardly wait until we returned to camp and I could show the note to Israel, the only one I could confide in.

Israel advised me against taking the offer since escape was an offense with the harshest consequences. Even if I weren't caught, I would jeopardize my family. It took little time for me to decide that I couldn't be that selfish.

I wrote a note back to Gertrude, explaining why I couldn't

accept her offer and asking her to visit my family if she ever went home on furlough. She accepted my reasoning and agreed to visit at her first opportunity.

Gertrude continued every day to bring me food, which I took and shared with Israel. Before long, however, I got a new assignment. Through his network, Haubenstock had learned of my sandwiches and had his first opportunity for revenge.

I was sent to the Bata Shoe Factory as a laborer, loading coal, cleaning up, and carrying boxes. The work was hard, but I didn't mind. My only fears were of injury or serious illness, and I was lucky enough to avoid both.

After I'd been at Bata for a couple of weeks, I was alone in an elevator with a German man whom I'd never seen before, and he handed me ration coupons for ten pounds of bread. This was a very serious offense, not only for me, but for the nice German. I don't know how Haubenstock learned of the incident, but that evening he appeared in our room and asked me to hand over the coupons. I did.

Nonetheless, the next morning, I was assigned to clear snow in nearby towns and villages. We marched out at dawn and returned at dusk after working all day in the bitter cold of February, 1942. Even this assignment, however, was not always terrible for me. On the days when the S.A. guards from Mangersdorf were with us, they ordered me to make a fire and keep it going for them. When Haubenstock got wind of that, I was left in camp, a punishment tantamount to starvation, since those who didn't work received more meager rations. Since Israel and I shared everything, I managed to get by, but being kept in camp, unable to be with my comrades and forced to combine Israel's full rations with my portion, made my life miserable. And I didn't dare write home for help, since I knew life there was sometimes more difficult than life in the forced labor camps.

I spent my days wandering around camp or in the company of other inmates. When Lux had daytime guard duty, he sometimes had me accompany him on his rounds. However, I never again complained to him about my lot. It wouldn't pay to antagonize Haubenstock and his minions again.

One day, Israel received a package from a friend named Nathan in Zurich, Switzerland. It contained a can of sardines and some chocolate. Israel had a girl friend in Bendin, whom he had known from the kibbutz. Her name was Sarah, and she had Aryan papers. She was a runner for the underground and in touch with Switzerland's Jewish organizations. Without our bidding, she had arranged for Israel to be sent the packages. Others followed, with the next couple also reaching him, but then the guards heard about them and started intercepting and confiscating them. They ended up in the hands of the S.A. commandant. Such attention was not desirable, so Israel got word to Sarah, and the packages from Zurich stopped coming.

Despite the difficulties of camp life, circumstances and our ingenuity kept it from being dull. One of our roommates was a Professor Weisner, a teacher. Several of us asked him to give us lessons. He consented, and, for an hour or two each evening, he talked of history, geography, literature, and myriad other subjects. His "lectures" became jumping-off points for discussions of the world and of life. Everyone who wanted to could participate. I listened eagerly, hungry to know of things I'd never had a chance to learn.

Josef, another of our roommates, was a married man from Sosnowitz. His separation from his family added a note of poignancy and perspective to our days. Once, I noticed him sitting on his bunk, crying, a card from home in his hand. I gave him time to calm down, and then went over to ask the reason for his tears. Everyone in camp had become used to bad news, and we sought, when we could, to soften the pain. He showed me the letter. His wife had written that their daughter of twelve had become a woman, experiencing her first menstrual period. He cried because, with the uncertainty of his life, he guessed he would never see them again and would never share, except at a distance, such milestones of their lives.

March came, and rumors developed that a group was to be

formed to start a new camp. I discussed this with Israel, telling him I was sick of sitting idle and worrying about what might happen to me next. I had decided to volunteer for transport to this unknown camp, I said. I had little to lose. He decided to come with me.

In the middle of the month, the rumors became reality. We were assembled. We had become like well-trained soldiers, forming into straight lines for the ritual of being counted by the S.A. and reporting to the commandant. That day there was a three-member civilian commission present. The one who seemed to be in charge—we dubbed him the "Horse Trader"—paused in front of me as he looked us over. My heart only stopped for a couple of seconds.

Pacing along our lines, he told us he was looking for tradesmen—carpenters, bricklayers, electricians, plumbers—to be the nucleus of a new camp in Silesia. We would later work there in a factory for the German Reich. He asked the tradesmen to step forward, which Israel and I did. About 140 of us volunteered. A fellow named Carl, from Vienna, was put in charge. He was later to become the Jewish elder of 5,000 inmates in the new Silesian camp.

We were told to pack so we could be ready to leave on five minutes' notice, and we were dismissed.

We speculated on where destiny was taking us. It was against my principles to volunteer, but now, not only had I stepped forward, I had also talked Israel into coming along. I took the full load on my shoulders: should things not work out, I would never forgive myself.

We packed before the performance by the inmates that was scheduled for that evening. Such spectacles were held about once a month, and were staged on a couple of days' notice. Whoever had any talent was enlisted to entertain the guards and their fellow-inmates with singing, dancing, magic, and other acts. We went to the show, but our minds were already in the new, unknown camp.

The next morning, in the still, cold March air, we volunteers lined up with our meager belongings. We were, as usual, counted and recounted, and then we were marched to the railway station. Again, I was waving goodbye to comrades I left behind, some of whom I was never to see again.

The march to the station took about twenty minutes. There we had to wait for about an hour for the train to arrive. It was a military train heading east, full of indestructible young soldiers and S.S. troops. Their good spirits were obvious in their devil-may-care attitude, their insolence, and their laughter. Many of them teased us, making fun of our column. Some threw insults and threats in our direction, but, since we were guarded by the S.A., these strong, handsome, arrogant young men couldn't do much to us.

At the back of the train, behind the passenger cars and their cargo of world conquerors, were three snow-covered cattle wagons, into which we were loaded. The ride, to a station called "Kozel" Silesia, took about three hours. There, we were unloaded, formed into a line, counted, recounted, and turned over to the Shutzpolizei. The S.A. men returned to Ottmuth. The train pulled out as the march to our new home began. In our ears echoed the parting taunts of the soldiers who continued toward the eastern front.

Z.A.L. Blechhammer

After marching about thirty minutes, we passed through the gates of our destination, under the sign "Zwangarbeits Lager Blechhammer." We stopped in the yard, exhausted, and threw down our belongings. It wasn't time to rest, however. We were again lined up and placed at attention, where we remained for an hour until the head of the Shutzpolizei favored us with his presence. The commandant, a tall, cruel-looking captain of about forty, who before the war had been an ordinary policeman in Bavaria, told us we were to work, work, and work, until we were dead.

"There is no other way out," he said. "Anybody trying to escape will be shot on the spot. Our victorious German army is on the outskirts of Moscow, Leningrad, and Stalingrad, and you must perform for the victory of the Reich."

The signal for dismissal was greeted with a sigh of relief. We were ready to collapse after a hectic day. We were assigned to barracks, which were brand new, still smelling of fresh wood. Farther into the woods was a large cleared area, ready for construction of hundreds of additional new barracks. Eventually, the camp would have 40,000 inmates from all of the captive nations of Europe.

Israel and I took a double bunk, I on the bottom. Several of our companions were ordered to the guards' kitchen, about a mile away, to get coffee, which they carried, two to a kettle, to our barracks. Food continued to be brought that way, through dirt or mud, by guarded inmates, until the camp

Israel (center), my dear friend, who was hanged for trying to escape from Buntzlau

kitchen was completed. We lined up for coffee, drank, and went to sleep.

The next morning, at five, assembly lights were turned on in the barracks and on the grounds. We had an hour to wash, have coffee, and get our meager daily rations before going to work. This became our daily routine, the only change being an increase in our numbers as additional recruits from other camps and towns joined us over the next few days. That first morning, the guards counted heads and set up work units. Israel and I were together.

It was still dark when we arrived at our work site. We learned that we were to build and prepare a factory and barracks for 40,000 slave laborers. The factory belonged to I. G. Farben and was to be named Herman Goering Werke. It would produce synthetic gasoline and various byproducts from coal.

Work was hard, though conditions depended somewhat on which group you had the luck to work in and on your foreman. Sometimes you worked under a nice human being, but most of the time you were controlled by a vicious devil.

I worked for a company that put in the water mains. Though it was grueling, it was in my chosen craft, so I couldn't complain. Israel, who had worked in bookkeeping with his father before joining the kibbutz, dug ditches.

We quickly fell into the routine, which included another element we could have done without. The commandant also rose early and would visit the wash barrack. He carried a bullwhip with a piece of lead attached to its tip, which he used to discipline the men. Anyone who washed with his clothes on, for example, got to bend over with his pants down and receive a minimum of twenty-five lashes. In some instances, the commandant and his whip crippled inmates permanently.

One evening, Carl the elder came to our room and asked me if I knew anything about electrical work. I told him the only connection I had with electricians was that I had worked with them in new buildings at various times. He asked if I could hold a screwdriver, because he had received orders to produce three electricians by the next morning. I agreed to become an electrician, figuring it would be easier than working with twelve-inch water pipes. Israel and Max, a man from Sosnowitz, became the other two electricians.

The next day, a German on a bicycle arrived and took the three of us with him. His name was Hans, and he was about thirty and was tall and blond. I wondered why a fellow like this was not serving in the army. I soon found out the factory was a very important war-related project, under the personal supervision of General Pohl, and Hans was too valuable there to send to battle.

At the construction site, Hans brought us to an old German and to a Pole named Frank. Frank was also a forced laborer, but under vastly different circumstances from ours. He was paid for his work and could go home once a month for three days. He could not, however, quit or seek other work.

Work began at 7:00 A.M. sharp. Hans laid a blueprint out in front of us. Luckily, I was accustomed to such plans and, after studying it for a while and roughing in one building—which was to be a barrack—I was able to do the others the same way. We worked in pairs. Israel and I worked together, and Max worked with Frank. The old German, whom we called "Father," had charge of materials and tools, which he gave us as needed.

We "electricians" were a happy threesome. We could move freely on the construction site. We had civilian clothes, with our only identification a Star of David sewn on our jackets in white yarn. When we took off our jackets, there was nothing to mark us as Jewish. After a week, we were far ahead of schedule, especially Israel and I, who became experts in expediting our work, as if we had done it all our lives. Hans frequently left us to ourselves, only appearing at quitting time to take us back to camp, where he saluted the camp commandant with a loud "Heil Hitler" before going off on his bicycle.

On many occasions, we used Hans's bicycle to joy ride through the construction site, which was huge. Israel, who was well educated and a talented writer, kept a diary on loose sheets of paper, recording everything. It made very good reading.

On one of my jaunts around the site, I discovered a Pole named Jan, whom I knew from Bendin. He had had a tobacco stand across from my father's butcher shop. I was glad to see his familiar face. He was a free worker, able to move about as much as he wished. Though of course he had to continue working for the Germans, he could have requested other assignments had he wanted to. He traveled home for the weekend every two weeks. I was in heaven when he said he would look up my parents and give them my regards. I thanked him for his thoughtfulness.

On the Monday after Jan's next trip home, my impatience was unbounded. I couldn't wait to get on Hans's bike and search the site. I soon found Jan at his working place. He had brought me a letter, a carrot cake, a potato cake and 200 hand-made cigarettes, rolled personally by my father.

The news from home wasn't encouraging. Mother was still

working for Rosner. Father got very little meat to distribute, being supplied, perhaps, once a month. Jack had been sent to forced labor at Ottmuth. Things in Bendin were getting worse daily.

The Germans were ordering people to resettle, allowing them ten kilograms of luggage, assembling them and shipping them to forced labor or liquidation camps. First, they took a thousand Jews. Their next demand was for 5,000. The Germans terrorized the officials of the Judenrat—the body of elders that supplied laborers—into submission, forcing them to comply.

No one appeared when they made their third demand for bodies, so the Germans, with the help of the Jewish police, made a raid in the middle of the night and took away all the Jews from an entire building, forty to fifty people. This was the first of a series of raids that helped decimate the area.

People began building shelters, hiding places in their apartments, where they could retreat to when there was a midnight knock at the door.

There was talk, serious talk, that a ghetto would be created and all the remaining Jews would be gathered there. This would be part of the "final solution" to the "Jewish problem" in Europe that was being directed by Reinhard Heydrich and his stooges. A ghetto would make it easier to catch, transport, and liquidate them. Jews imprisoned in ghettos would have minimum control over their own fates. They would be waiting only for a final deportation, their destinies sealed.

The letter depressed me. It was a portent of what was about to happen and I was helpless.

Meanwhile, I was now a veteran of eighteen months of incarceration—an oldtimer. Life in camp was hell for everybody. The commandant was vicious. He continued pre-dawn visits to the wash barrack, leaving quite a few of my comrades crippled. The camp population had grown to 600 Jews, and the guard force included a few Wehrmacht soldiers from the Russian front who could no longer perform front line duties.

On Jan's next trip, I sent a letter asking Father and Sam to volunteer for a forced-labor camp, which would be much safer than being rounded up and deported for resettling in a place such as Auschwitz. We, in our camp, had heard of that hell and could not believe its horrors.

Through my letters, Israel's family was informed of our whereabouts, and, one day in June, his sister, Lola, appeared at our construction site. She carried fake Aryan papers and had managed to get a travel permit to visit her boyfriend at the Herman Goering Werke. We arranged for Israel to see her for an hour in private with the help of the German "Father," who also spoke a little Polish.

I later found out they were planning an escape. Months later, in October, she brought him money and a letter from his girl friend, Sarah. His plans were made in secret, hidden even from me. He didn't want to get me involved, since that would get me in trouble if he were caught.

I maintained my connection to home through Jan, and more bad news came with each letter. Grandma was deported, destination unknown. Mama and Papa received a box of ashes from Auschwitz with a letter saying Mother's brother, Mayer, had died of a heart attack. He was thirty-five and had been strong as a mule and never sick in his life.

In my camp, we got a Lagerfuehrer named Hoffman. A native of Munich, Bavaria, he was a civilian in charge of administrative functions and worked with the military commandant. We called him "Moses the Rooster," since he was tall and slim with a pointed head. He was long-time party man and always wore his party insignia in his lapel.

Hoffman was ruthless. He and the commandant, the "Master of the Ritual Bath," were an awesome pair to cope with, each striving to be more brutal than the other, and so we suffered. We were hit by both. They said to each other: "If you beat up my Jews, I will beat up yours."

Hoffman took a Jewish girl from Sosnowitz as his personal "chambermaid." She was young, pretty, and inexperienced. She became pregnant, so Hoffman put her on the first transport to Auschwitz, where she died in a gas chamber. Hoffman was to be tried in Munich after the war and receive ten years' hard labor for his crimes against humanity. Carl the Elder and I would be present for his trial.

Considering the circumstances, we electricians had it pretty good. When life in camp became too unbearable, we asked Hans if we could work on Sundays, too. He wrote to the head office of Siemens and Schuckert, the electrical contractor for the site, which had to pay for our work, and was given permission for our extra hours. We were very glad. We avoided our commandant's sadism, the cleaning of latrines and grounds, and merciless pushups and other exercises, done to a point where some of the workers were left on the ground unconscious. We also got an extra bowl of soup because we worked on Sundays for the German Reich.

In July of 1942, a diphtheria epidemic broke out in Blechhammer. The Germans sealed off the camp. We were locked up for three weeks, not knowing what was going to happen. Even the guards didn't come into camp; they were afraid of us. Though disease stalked us, in a way, we were glad.

By that time, we had our own kitchen. The guards remained on the perimeter of the camp. Their only contact with us was passing food to us through the barbed-wire fence.

Our German co-worker "Father" came to the barbed wire daily to see Israel, Max, and me. He had become kind of attached to us. He would pace around outside the fence, waiting for a chance to talk. The first day, we spoke for only a few minutes, since we didn't want to put him in jeopardy. The next day, he brought us eight pounds of farmer's bread and gave us his cigarette rations. He promised to return again the next day.

We prepared letters home, and "Father" mailed them, risking his life. We later found out that our parents had gotten the mail.

Finally, the quarantine was lifted, and the camp, its population somewhat smaller because of a few deaths due to the disease, resumed its routine.

A month later, a camp assembly was held, and about half of us were told to disperse, pack and reassemble in an hour, ready to march.

Israel, my dear friend, and I were separated. We embraced and wished each other luck. He, Max, and several other of my friends, were sent to a forced-labor camp named Buntzlaw. There, he finally attempted his escape, but he was captured and killed. Before he left Blechhammer, he put the pages of his diary in a sheet-metal box and buried them. They may still rest on the site of that camp.

Z.A.L. Brande

I was sent to a camp called Brande, along with about a hundred other inmates of Blechhammer. We arrived after an uneventful train ride and were counted, standing at attention before our new commandant, a sour-looking man with a wooden leg, who was dressed in the black uniform of the organization Totd, the engineers corps, with an armband displaying the twisted cross. His left leg had been amputated because of wounds suffered fighting in Poland. He carried a bullwhip, which he used at any excuse to prove his meanness. Though he was a Wehrmacht officer, the rest of the guards were Shupo.

He surveyed us carefully, and then singled me out, signaling me to step forward. I cringed inwardly, thinking of the bullwhip reaching out for my body. I stood motionless, at attention. He looked me over some more, then told me to come to the guardhouse the next morning. I was to be given special duties. I didn't know what to say or expect. Reflexively, I yelled, "*Jawohl!*" (yes, sir).

We were dismissed and sent to another collection of prefab wooden barracks. Many of my companions congratulated me, expressing envy because it appeared I would have inside work and, perhaps, extra food. After I was assigned a berth, I wandered around the barrack, and discovered my uncle Mordekai from Sosnowitz among my companions, whose family I had stopped with when I returned from my brief army service. He had made a good living as a furniture polisher before the war. After we embraced, he told me Brande was a small transit camp with a high turnover of prisoners. There were about four hundred inmates. Those who were put to work, worked hard for twelve hours a day with rations approaching the starvation level—not enough to live on, but not enough to die on, either. He had been in Brande for six months and didn't know where his wife and twelve-year-old redhaired daughter, my cousin, were. Even years later, I was unable to find out what happened to them.

Mordekai said that almost daily he exchanged his ration of bread for tobacco, which was a sure way to commit suicide. While he was just fulfilling a habit, not actively trying to die, all my efforts to talk him into living were in vain.

Our first full day in Brande, the morning assembly was called at six, and columns of prisoners were counted and marched off to work. I was told to see the camp commandant, whom we called the "Lame Duck."

I knocked at the door. "Herein" (come in) came the answer. I marched in and stood at attention until the Lame Duck told me to be at ease.

He told me I was to be his butler. My duties were to keep the fire going at all times, clean his boots (though he had one leg, he had two boots), clean and brush his clothes, keep his room shipshape, and bring his meals from the kitchen to his quarters.

There was always food left over on his tray from which I could make a decent meal. My regular ration I shared with my uncle, prolonging his life as much as I could. He still died within six months of my finding him.

My "good life" of keeping the Lame Duck happy lasted about four weeks. Then, one afternoon I walked in unexpectedly and surprised him with a suitcase full of gold coins and jewelry open on the table. There was no question in my mind where it had come from. He was furious at my intrusion and ordered me to leave and not return. I was finished working for him. Jarosh, the Jewish elder, personally brought me the news that the next day I was to join the working force like everyone else.

I feared that his anger would cost me my life, and worked

at the various heavy labor assignments I was given for the next six weeks with fear as my constant companion. At the end of that time, a commission arrived to pick slave laborers for another new camp, and I was the first to volunteer. The head of the commission was once more the "Horse Trader" who had sought craftsmen when I was at Ottmuth. I now found out that he was named Haushild. I tried to look my best as he studied us and came forward when he said he needed electricians. Even an unknown camp sounded better to me than a camp in which I was on the commandant's blacklist. I felt it was extremely dangerous for me to stay in Brande.

Thus, I put another camp behind me and again let the unknown future fill my mind. I stayed awake all that night, the events of the past three camps running around and around in my memory. I resolved to watch my step in the future and to remain inconspicuous. It only took one slip to become a dead pigeon.

Z.A.L. Sagan

The next morning, those of us who were leaving attended camp assembly as usual and watched those who were staying at Brande march off to work. We were ordered to draw an extra day's ration—about one pound of bread and a small piece of margarine—and be ready to march within the hour.

It was early November, 1942. The days were growing shorter; they were rainy and progressively colder, and our clothes were wearing out with no replacements in sight.

We were formed into a column and, guarded by the Schutzpolizei, marched to the railway station, where we had to wait for two hours until our train arrived. It was a passenger train, but it pulled three enclosed cattle wagons, into which we were loaded, after being counted. We learned that our destination was Zwangarbeits Lager Sagan. The guards told us this was a brand-new camp and was not far from Berlin. Now, I thought, we will be in the heart of Germany; it will be very difficult to communicate with anyone at home.

The train ride lasted overnight, and, when we disembarked the next morning, we were marched for fifteen or twenty minutes to our new address. I was honored to open my third new camp, this time as part of a hundred-man nucleus.

At Sagan, we were quickly formed into four columns. We stood at attention before the camp commandant, a Shupo lieutenant in his mid to late fifties, whose gray hair topped a face that held piercing blue eyes that tried to look through each of us. He marched as if he were on parade, with a troop of honor guards. Into his entourage went the camp's *Juden Altester* (Jewish elder), a man named to the post on the train. We were counted by a Shupo, who saluted and reported: "One hundred Jews present and accounted for."

The commandant spoke: "You are here to work for Germany, and especially for the German railway. Since there is a war, anybody not performing properly will be considered a saboteur, and sabotage is punishable by death. You should be proud to be alive and working for the great German Reich because the wheels must roll for victory."

We were dismissed and sent to barracks, again a set of prefabs of freshly cut lumber. Each room contained twenty double bunks, each bunk with its sack filled with straw and a blanket from military surplus. As usual, the grounds were fenced and overlooked by four watchtowers, each with a guard and some dogs.

This time, however, the kitchen, as well as the guard barrack, was outside the barbed wire. Only the wash barrack and our private outhouses with their six to ten positions were at our disposal. We ate in our rooms.

I went to shower and, refreshed, also washed my shirts and underwear. I still was reasonably well supplied with clothes, under the circumstances, having received additional underwear, a sweater, socks and shirts from home through various messengers. I carried these carefully, still in the plywood case I had brought to the orphanage from my physical examination so many months before. I felt good for that moment, clean and relatively relaxed. One key to survival was to stay as clean as possible. In a clean body, I knew, there is a clean soul; in a healthy body is a healthy soul. Many more of my comrades would have survived by keeping clean.

On our first morning in Sagan, we were assembled at 5:00 A.M.; no one could say we were late sleepers. We received an excuse for coffee and 200 grams of rock-hard black bread, made with a mixture of flour and sawdust. This, with an occasional small offering of marmalade, was to be our usual breakfast, and our lunch. Then we formed the usual lines, were counted and recounted, and formed into groups of twenty. A foreman was named for each group. Two camp inmates were named colony leaders. The colony leaders were with us all day on any job site, overseeing our activities. The foremen provided a working tempo for their groups. The elder remained in camp to do office work. The Germans were very precise about bookkeeping. Someone was paid for our work so records had to be meticulous.

Among the various appointed leaders were many who worked hard to please the Germans, becoming as cruel as our guards. Later, when we were interned in concentration camps, the additional position of "capo" would be filled. These men, named by the camp elders, were in charge of meting punishment to their fifty-man colonies. They seemed to be chosen for meanness and tended to be strong and loudmouthed. Some of them were good, fair, and temperate, but most sought to out-Nazi the Germans. Everyone in these layers of leadership was trying to save his own skin, seeking easier work, extra food, generally better conditions for himself. Still, I could take abuse from the Germans far more easily than I could from those of my own faith. We hated them far more than we hated the Germans.

At the work site, our groups of twenty were subdivided into work details as needed. Over each detail was a uniformed railway supervisor from the German Reich. Our main job was to pack stones under wooden railroad ties with pickhammers. We worked for eleven hours, pausing only for an hour at noon to eat what was left of the 200 grams of bread we had received in the morning. Coffee was cooked on the construction site. It tasted like mud. When we returned to camp at night, we were served soup that was made of scraps brought to camp in paper bags labeled "only for Jews and pigs." New arrivals, who came into camp healthy and relatively well fed, wouldn't eat the food we toughened veterans ate with gusto, if not relish. But they learned to eat or they sickened, and that meant death. Indeed, after two or three days in camp, the newcomers would beg us to return the soup they had earlier given away. Naturally, we couldn't. It was a matter of survival.

Sagan was a strategic interchange through which all war materiel and soldiers had to go to the eastern front. The rails were in constant use and required constant care. We saw panzers, and blond, laughing soldiers on the way to the Russian front. Had they known what awaited them, I doubt they would have laughed. The young, especially, laughed spiritedly; they were the elite troops of the S.S. Some looked at us with pity. Some even threw us half-smoked or scarcely started cigarettes.

We had many casualties at our job site. After a short time, our numbers were reinforced by 100 new workers, shipped by train fresh from home through a transit camp at Sosnowitz. Their numbers were quickly depleted and, within two weeks of their arrival, fifty of them were unable to work because of injury or refusal to eat caused by depression.

The sick were left in camp, and, if they didn't recover within a few days, they were transported east to the gas chambers of Auschwitz, the death camp established under the auspices of the S.S. Auschwitz, which was under the command of Rudolph Hess, former manager of Sachsenhausen, another concentration camp. It had received its first victims in June, 1940, among them my uncle, Mayer. At Sagan, candidates for Auschwitz were created at a rate of twenty-five a week. I often wondered how long it would be before I joined that parade.

We returned to camp each evening exhausted, without any breath left. I always went to the wash barracks as soon as we were dismissed. Others fell on their bunks unable to move, but that was like giving up without a fight. Then came supper, a bowl of that bitter, watery soup. Some of us were too exhausted to eat; some couldn't stand the taste. Having nothing else, I was glad to warm my guts. Besides, it probably contained some vitamins.

Several weeks after the opening of Sagan, I was ordered at assembly to report immediately to the commandant, who asked if I was an electrician. I said I was, adding that I had worked as a foreman for Siemens and Schuckert. This seemed to impress him. I could see him smiling. He told me that from then on I was to report to Mr. Krieger; I was to do important work for the Reich.

The next day, I met Krieger, who told me my job was to lay underground cables, splice together the multiple wires, and put a lead cover over the spliced sections to protect the joints from the elements. I promised I would do my best. I was also to pick ten other inmates to dig the ditches along the train route into which the cable would go. Somebody above watched over me as I was again taken away from the heaviest work in my camp, having, for a while, relatively easy work that let me breathe at a normal pace.

Krieger turned out to be a very decent German. He began to give me, indirectly, bits of food: a couple of baked potatoes, a leftover sandwich, and, some days, an apple. Occasionally, he brought a couple of German cigarettes, which tasted very good if I smoked them or which I could exchange for a full portion of bread with the leaders of the camp, who always managed to get extra rations.

As a rapport developed between us, Krieger told me many Germans were against the war and the killings. But, he asked, "What can we do, and with what?" He was even afraid to talk in front of his family, since his children were fanatical Nazis, members of the Hitler Youth, their minds poisoned by the system.

Reinforcements from home arrived as needed to keep the camp work force up to quota. Transports left for Auschwitz as needed. After several weeks, a batch of newcomers arrived that included someone who could give me news of home: Judith's brother Elie. He brought me up to date on the plight of those who remained in Bendin. He told me everyone in the Jewish parts of the city was in constant danger of being hunted down, captured, beaten, shot or transported. Some of them even envied those of us who had learned to survive camp life. Elie told me that Papa and my youngest brother, Sam, who was then thirteen, were sent to camp in "Kletendorf." Mother was still working for Rosner and was still exempt from deportation. She sought to stay at home in case somehow she could help us in camp.

At the beginning of 1943, the Germans formed the last of the ghettos they would create in occupied territory at Bendin, limiting the movement and living space of the Jews to the area which was once my home. Thus, Mother was able to continue to live at home until the final liquidation of the ghetto in August, 1943. Until then, her life went as could be expected under the circumstances. She shared our apartment with my Aunt Ida, the wife of one of Father's brothers. Ida had been considered wealthy before the invasion, she and her husband running a bakery and two pastry shops. When the rest of her family was transported, she moved in with Mother.

Despite the extra food I received from Mr. Krieger, my fondest dream each night was of dying with a full stomach. I never knew hunger could hurt so much, with your guts playing a march inside your body. I could imagine how bad it must have been for my companions who had nothing extra.

As Christmas neared, we began counting the hours until we would get an extra day of rest. On Christmas Eve, a special and unexpected treat developed. I happened to be walking around the grounds when a Shupo whom we called "The Terrible" crossed the area. In each camp, there was one guard who was particularly vicious. In Sagan, he was the one. He walked around, making use of his bullwhip with our without reason, and who was going to tell him to stop beating up Jews? When he motioned me over that evening, I trembled. He displayed to me a crow he had shot earlier and gave it to me for Christmas. Disbelieving my senses, I thanked him and told him it was my birthday. "Happy Birthday," he said, and I, in turn, wished him a Merry Christmas.

I took this new prize and carried it quickly into the barracks. There were thirty-nine pairs of eyes staring at me as I hustled in. My roommates gathered around to hear what had happened, incredulous that I was given this gift by The Terrible. They asked if I were going to cook it, asking for a bone or leftover soup if I did.

My ideas were more elaborate. Outside the fence at the back of the camp were tons of potatoes, piled in small mounds and covered with straw and dirt until they were to be used. I decided that, while the guards were celebrating, I would add some of those delicacies to our feast.

At eleven o'clock, I walked outside. There was only one guard at the main gate, a Shupo in his sixties, who stood cursing his luck at being out in the cold while everyone else was busy drinking. I kept him company for a while, talking with him about the holiday as if I were an expert on Christmas. After all, I thought, wasn't Christ a Jew whose birthday these Nazis celebrated even as they justified their brutality to us by charging we were "Christ-killers"? After we talked about the holy day for awhile, I wished him a Merry Christmas and wandered off along the twelve-foot–high fence topped with strands of barbed wire supported on inward-thrusting poles. I walked slowly, watching for any sign of another guard. There was none, so I gathered a laundry sack, strolled to a fence pole at the back of the compound as far from the guard barrack as possible, and climbed over. I filled the sack with twenty-five to thirty pounds of potatoes—enough for each of my roommates to have at least one—then threw the sack into the camp and followed it back over the fence. I buried the sack in the air-raid shelter that was inside the camp and strolled back to our room, breathing a sigh of relief when I was again safe inside.

On Christmas Day, we awoke early, full of happiness at having a crow and a large sack of potatoes to cook. Everyone was sworn to secrecy and promised a share in the loot.

We gathered the potatoes with the laundry, cleaned the bird, and made a fire using powdered coal briquettes. We could cook openly since the guards knew about my Christmas gift. We shared the work of preparing the crow and finally had it safely in a pot of boiling water. We checked it every few minutes, since it was important to make sure it turned out well. Imagine: forty cooks, each a bigger expert than the next, and I had priority, since the bird was mine.

In the meantime, we buried our potatoes in the ashes, baking them as I had as a child on Grandpa's farm. Some of us couldn't wait and ate raw potatoes but, baked or half-baked, they filled our stomachs.

So we were busy, cooking and eating. The crow meat, instead of getting softer, became harder by the minute. I became very disappointed, having dreamed all night of eating the first meat I'd had in a long time. Finally, I got disgusted with the waiting. I took the bird out of the pot and cut it into small pieces. I took a leg. It was like a piece of leather, but who cared? At least it smelled better than the grass we received daily. In any event, we had a better Christmas than we had expected.

The next day, we went back to work. We noticed that the number of weapons and troops being transported east was increasing. The army at Stalingrad was about to be surrounded and decisively defeated.

Also increasing was the number of wounded Germans on their way to hospitals. These young soldiers no longer joked and laughed at our expense. They were depressed and in pain, with bullet wounds and gangrene infecting frostbitten noses, ears, and limbs. They had their own troubles and left us alone. Some still threw cigarettes to us, but their attitude had changed. The taunting was gone, seemingly replaced by some awareness of humanity and human frailty. The sight of the injured also tempered the attitude of the healthy young men who were replacing them at the front, making the whole atmosphere at the interchange more morbid. We took silent pleasure in seeing what was happening.

In the woods near Sagan, five to ten kilometers farther from the railroad than we were, was a cluster of prisoner-of-war camps holding captured combatants from the allied nations. Many of them were air force people. The POWs were kept isolated from us laborers at Sagan, though they were sometimes impressed into working. Every day, the higher-ranked officers were taken for walks in groups of four or five by their Luftwaffe guards. These prisoners looked at us with pity. Most of them were English or French. We knew this by the cigarettes they sometimes threw in our direction, which were Gitanes or Players.

The week between Christmas and New Year's Day was agonizingly cold but still filled with hard work: digging ditches with picks and shovels in the frozen ground. Our goal had become to make it to New Year's Day, another extra day of rest with, perhaps, a little extra food. The hunger was unbearable for most of us. It was common for inmates to scrounge stealthily through the garbage, looking for the leavings from the guards' tables. While we were given marginal fare, the guards ate well. While there were some prize leavings found, more often inmates settled for the rotten outer leaves from cabbage heads and similar waste. Quite a few of the prisoners who partook became ill, their faces, eyelids, legs, and arms swollen by infection. They became the next candidates for transport to Auschwitz.

On New Year's Eve, our room elder, a man named Silberman, who was from Wadowitz, near Krakow, decided to do what I had done on Christmas Eve. He was a decent man in his late twenties who avoided hurting those in his charge as much as he could. All of the elders and leaders behaved meanly; they had to, to work with the Germans. The ones who just yelled at us, rather than hitting, were the decent ones. Silberman scouted the perimeter of the camp, went over the fence, and filled a sack with potatoes. His luck ran out, however, as he returned to the compound. He was spotted by a Shupo, who brought him and his bulging sack before the commandant, who was furious. He ordered an immediate, middle-of-the-night search of all rooms and bunks. Instead of a day of rest, we were assigned work in camp. That day at assembly, we were formed into a circle around a bench and held at attention. Silberman, the criminal, was brought forward, put face down on the bench and given fifty lashes across his bare buttocks with us watching. I shuddered as I visualized myself on that bench being scored by a lead-tipped bullwhip. Silberman's buttocks were a mass of frozen blood when the whipping ended, and he could not lie on his back for three weeks, but the next day he had to go to work as usual. Yet his punishment was light because his brother was a colony leader.

My job splicing cable was completed, and I was given a new assignment. The local electrical contractor was a staff sergeant on the Waffen S.S. who was on leave from the eastern front. He needed an electrician to install wiring in a new barrack for forced laborers, and I was to be that electrician.

He said nothing to me except what was necessary for the job. We worked inside the new building first, and he told me that, after finishing that part of the job, we had to run five hundred meters of wire outside on twenty-foot poles to bring in the power. The weather was rainy and cold when we started that phase of the job, just right to encase everything in ice. As I tried to scale the first pole, I lost my grip on the cold sheath and slipped to the ground. He bawled me out for my clumsiness and went to climb the pole himself, learning firsthand the problems involved. Sharing the problem helped widen the line of communication between us.

He began to leave sandwiches in a corner of the barrack where I would find them when I cleaned up. Then, in our third week together, he started talking to me about the war. Knowing my audience, I drew a picture of the German effort so rosy that even the most partisan expert couldn't have done better. He opened up more and more, but he still didn't hand me the food he left for me. I still had to pick it up from the floor, but I didn't mind. It helped me survive. He was very proud of me and my work, but I never learned his name. I called him *Oberscharfuehrer;* in Germany then, everyone was some kind of a *Fuehrer*.

The first week in February, the Germans gave up their attack on Stalingrad. My boss discussed this with me. It was on his mind since he had been on the eastern front and might have to return there. I suggested the move was probably strategic retreat, designed to straighten out the line and keep the front intact, but deep in my heart I hoped that retreat, and the landing of allied forces in Tunisia, which took place at about the same time, was the beginning of the Reich's end.

Since my comments agreed with my S.S. man's thoughts, he liked me more and became even more talkative. Finally, in my desperation, I gathered my courage and asked him if he would be so kind as to visit my parents' home. I hadn't heard of them in a long time. I told him his expenses from Sagan would, of course, be reimbursed with something extra, perhaps some schnapps, which was generally in short supply. He said he had to think it over. Perhaps my concern and urgency came through. Perhaps I was more persuasive than I believed possible. Whatever the reason, a short time later, he asked me to write down my parents' address. I couldn't believe it. This avowed Nazi was agreeing to take a 1,000-kilometer round trip to satisfy my desires. My heart beat faster. There was no way I could hide my joy. Still, my happiness was tempered. I felt I had finally re-established, at least temporarily, a live link with home, but I remained somewhat jittery about the messenger. And I was unsure what he would find at Mother's address. I worried about whether she was still at the apartment. I knew things had changed there, and I didn't expect any material gifts, but a letter from Mother would bolster me, reviving my courage to go on fighting to survive. That will to survive was all I really had. To reach a time beyond the war was my dream; the life I was living was my nightmare.

    I wrote a letter in German. I didn't want to write in Jewish and appear to be hiding something from my messenger. I wrote of my life, making it sound better than it was, and said how lucky I was to be working as a tradesman most of the time. I had it much better than the others, I added. I didn't realize it then but this would be my last connection with home, my last letter from Mother and her last loving package.

    When the S.S. man left for the weekend, I knew he would see my mother. That was one thing about the Germans: they kept their promises. The weekend took forever. I couldn't sleep, imagining him at the front door talking to Mother, telling her about my work with him. I prayed things would be all right.

    On Tuesday, he was back. He told me things were very bad in general and for the Jews in particular. He had brought me a package, which he put in the camp chimney after the wash water was heated for the day and the fire was out. I was to pick it up so nobody would see me, not even my roommates. He bawled me out, half-jokingly, complaining that for this "shit" he had traveled a thousand kilometers and spent almost two days on the train. That "shit" was to me manna from heaven. There was a letter in Yiddish, the last words I would have from my dear mother. The package contained a pair of Papa's old pants, a new pair of high shoes, a couple of shirts, some underwear, a carrot cake, and a potato cake. I never knew so much joy as from that new pair of shoes. They were so timely. Without them I would have been in big trouble. I hadn't realized how worn my old shoes were, but shortly after the package arrived, their soles came apart and there was no way to fix them at Sagan.

The trip to Bendin was also timely. Mother wrote that the ghetto was actively being formed. Around her, there was only pain and misery. Food was scarce but could still be bartered for. Everyone was being moved to the ghetto. She, too, was to move soon. In fact, had my messenger been a week later, she would have been gone.

I read the letter over and over, feeling Mother's agony and her love. I cried quietly long after all the other inmates were sound asleep.

The snow began to melt. At the end of March I finished my work with the S.S. man. I never saw him again. I was sent back to Mr. Krieger to dig more ditches and pull more cable along another section of the rails.

Late one morning at the beginning of April, I noticed a woman strolling back and forth near our ditch. It seemed very suspicious. I happened to be near her and asked if she were looking for somebody. She told me she had come from Bendin and had a package for Elie, Judith's brother. She was a Volksdeutscher, she said, and had known Elie's father before the war. While we spoke, a Shupo came over and asked what I was talking to this woman about. I told him she had walked by and I had asked if she could spare some bread since we were hungry. The woman was taken into custody, and she and I were escorted back to camp. I knew I had committed a terrible offense.

On that day, Sagan had an unexpected guest, Sturmbahnfuehrer Lindner, a major under Col. Adolph Eichmann in the branch of the S.S. charged with eliminating the Jews of Europe. Lindner was the man who chose, from the 500,000 Jews in Silesia, who was to live and who was to be gassed. He was the man who greeted prisoners at the camps and on a whim, pointed his thumb left, to death, or right, to slave labor.

We were taken to the camp administrative offices, outside the barbed-wire fence. The woman was taken for questioning first while I was put in a waiting area outside the commandant's office. She told her questioners that she was a German on the way to Berlin for the funeral of a relative who had died of wounds received at the eastern front. She said she had paused to sleep in Sagan because her journey was too tiring, and I had asked if she could spare some bread before the Shupo came over.

She was released, which was a slight relief to me because it meant they had believed her, and all I had to do was stick to my story. She left, taking the package for Elie, which was never to be delivered.

Then I was marched into the office. The commandant sat at his desk, which was bare but for a telephone, but I was marched before a chair in which a stranger sat. Later I would find out it was Lindner. I stood at attention. The room was hazy about me. All I could see was a red face under a black hat with a skull affixed to it. On each side of me stood an S.S. man with a bullwhip ready to be used. I was petrified.

"Do you know this woman?" Lindner asked.

My answer was no.

I felt the whips immediately, swung across my back, one-two, one-two, until Lindner signaled the men to stop. I didn't open my mouth despite the pain. I wouldn't give them the satisfaction of making me cry out.

"Did you speak to the woman?"

"Yes."

I noticed the bullwhips didn't go into action. They were only used when my answers were negative.

"What did you speak about?"

"I asked her if she could spare some bread."

The bullwhips went into action again.

"Do you know Auschwitz?"

I said no. I didn't lie, though the whips struck.

"Have you heard about Auschwitz?"

"Yes."

"Now, you go outside for five minutes and when you come back in you tell me the truth, or you'll be picked up and sent to Auschwitz."

All my blood rushed to my face as I walked out. As I stood waiting to be summoned again, a thousand thoughts ran through my mind. All the suffering and the effort to survive—for nothing? Maybe I should go over the fence. I had nothing to lose. I knew there was no way out of Auschwitz once you were sent there as punishment. I gathered my wits, preparing to face the black-hatted major again. When I was called inside, I addressed him as Herr Obersturmbahnfuehrer, promoting him to a colonel. I figured it couldn't hurt; after all, what is there to be disliked about being called "colonel" instead of "major"? The stakes I played for were my life.

Our tableau resumed, with me standing stiffly, he seated and the two whip-bearers always ready. He repeated his questions, again and again—a dozen times toying with me, and each time I gave the same answers. I was only hit whenever my answer was "no," even if that was the truth. After an hour of this, which seemed a lifetime, I was told to return to my barrack.

That evening, the commandant, accompanied by the camp elder, came to my barrack and assembled us, each by his bunk. He stood before me and, in an official, matter-of-fact tone, told me that Lindner had dressed him down because of me but that he had told Lindner I was the best electrician in camp and asked that he be lenient with me.

My bunk mates were relieved but I remained jittery that night. Although the commandant's words had put me a little bit at ease, I figured the true test would come the next morning. If they let me go to work as usual, there was a chance I was not bound for Auschwitz. I received that reassurance when I awoke and resumed a normal day's routine.

I told Mr. Krieger the story and asked if he could help me in case I decided to escape. "There is no escape," he replied, pointing out that I was in the heart of Germany, surrounded by checkpoints and without papers. I couldn't move more than a mile without being caught.

Two weeks went by. I had nearly buried my memories of the encounter with Lindner when suddenly I was called before the commandant and told to pack and be ready to leave within an hour. I didn't know what to make of it. When the time came to leave, I was joined by another inmate, who also worked as an electrician. A Shupo came for us, and we were walked to the railway station and put aboard a military passenger train.

We sat quietly for the most part. My comrade, Abe, tried to determine our destination, but the Shupo would not answer. We lapsed into silence. I knew we were heading east from the signs on the stations. We even got some cigarettes, volunteered by a Wehrmacht soldier headed for the eastern front, who threw them on the floor near us. The Shupo looked aside so we could pick them up.

Finally, the train stopped, and we were told to take our belongings. We walked for about half an hour, finally arriving at a camp site: it was the camp I had been at in March, 1941, Blechhammer. I was glad it was not Auschwitz.

K.Z. Blechhammer/Auschwitz III

Blechhammer was unrecognizable. When I had left, there had been a few hundred Jews confined there, most of them Polish. Now there were 5,000 Jews from all over Europe. The facility was on its way to becoming a concentration camp, though it was still run by the Shutzpolizei. Terrorism flourished, rations were less, the work harder. Capos had replaced foreman in the inmate hierarchy, being responsible for control rather than work. Eventually, each inmate was stripped of his belongings and whatever shreds of his dignity remained, becoming permanently a number marked with a tattoo.

Carl was still the Jewish elder with a Dutch Jew named Niven as his deputy. Our Shupo guard delivered us to the *Lagenfuehrer*, Hoffman. He and the *Lager* commandant, still the "bath master," looked us over. Hoffman recognized me, giving a low whistle that brought Carl to attention.

"Our electrician is back," Hoffman told him, acknowledging the return of a hard worker to his camp. "Give him good quarters and see to it he is made as comfortable as possible."

Somebody was watching over me. If this was supposed to be my punishment camp, it had backfired. Since Abe and I had arrived at midday, we had the rest of the day off. I was allowed to go to the guard's kitchen for an extra ration of bread and soup, and soup of a better quality than was made for the prisoners. The chef was an old friend of mine from Ottmuth, and so I ate a good, leisurely meal.

In the time I was away from Blechhammer, the factory

that was the heart of the area had begun operating and was turning out products from coal whenever it could be run. Since it had become a target of regular bombings by the allied forces, this production was not continuous. These bombings became more frequent as the summer passed, with the Royal Air Force attacking at night and the United States Air Corps during the day. Despite the attacks, the factory was expanding, and output of gasoline and of other products, such as margarine, saccharine, and pressed bricks of coal powder, increased. Nothing was wasted.

The heart of the factory was the *Kraftwerk*—power station—which was where I was assigned to work. While the factory was run by I.G. Farben, it was operated by Siemens-Halske, an electrical company. My boss was a furloughed Wehrmacht corporal who had been wounded in action on the eastern front. The assignment once again let me breathe a little freer.

Life was less pleasant for the other prisoners. Much of the work at Blechhammer was heavy. The camp was, indeed, a punishment colony and the general life expectancy of anyone sent there was short. All of us had to work diligently, with our main goal being to survive.

The inmates of Blechhammer represented all the captive countries of Europe, a kind of oppressed League of Nations. Transports traveled there from everywhere in Europe. The going became steadily rougher. In late August, a transport arrived from Bendin. Among the passengers was our school principal, a highly intelligent man. He was assigned to my room. He told me that the Bendin ghetto had been liquidated, with all the Jews in the area caught. My whole family, what had remained of it, had either been sent to labor camps or deported to Auschwitz. People once happy and strong had become like Musselmen. All were depressed by the Nazi device of separating families, a mode of warfare designed to destroy a person's will. Many people ceased to care, and, once on that road, their destination was destruction.

Among the camp inmates were collaborators, strongarm men who were only interested in improving their daily lot.

They had always been present, often as foremen and elders, but they were becoming more numerous and more desperate for their own survival. Many of them at that time were Jews, though, as more non-Jewish prisoners were mixed into the camp, the proportion changed. Criminals, political prisoners, and homosexuals became part of the camp population, and those who helped the Germans, though still prisoners, received somewhat better treatment and food and, they thought, a better chance to survive. These collaborators were the tools of the hierarchy in all the camps and seemed to feel they had to prove that they could be even worse than the Germans. There were also plenty of stool pigeons, so everyone had to be on guard. You had to be careful with whom you talked and what you talked about.

Another group arrived from Bendin near the end of September. It carried parents and their little children. Since we had no children in Blechhammer, they were all destined to be taken on to Auschwitz. One woman went to Carl and asked him to let her stay in Blechhammer, just having her child sent on. This was within his authority as elder.

She pleaded with him. Carl, who I had known since Ottmuth to be an honest and decent man, responded with a vehemence that shocked me.

"You whore!" he said. "You fucked to have this child. You go with him."

The child was a boy of about five, pretty and with a quality of innocence. My heart bled for him. I was not shaken by Carl's decision, but the way he handled the woman disappointed me greatly. His anger was so unexpected. It bred in me a dislike for Carl that lasted from then on.

Blechhammer became like Grand Central Station. There were always people passing through, many the remnants of the populations of towns that had all but ceased to exist. Life became harder for us more permanent inmates. Sunday ceased to exist as our rest day, as many of us were selected for camp cleanup work, which was many times worse than our regular construction assignments. Some of the cleanup work was necessary, though distasteful, like cleaning the wash barracks, digging out the outhouses, and raking the grounds, but some of the work, such as digging ditches and filling them back in, was totally without purpose. Always, as we labored, there were guards supervising, ready to punish any malingering.

Near our compound was a women's camp, which had been built while I was away. Barbed wire separated us from its few hundred prisoners. Their main duties were cooking and cleaning for the guards, cooking for the prisoners and washing and mending inmates' underwear and shirts. They provided full laundry service for the guards, who punished them randomly. Sometimes, women, and men, were punished just for their looks.

Evenings, I spent talking with fellow-Jews from France, Holland, Belgium and other parts of Europe. I was curious about their lives before the war, and learned that these men from Western Europe had been much better off than we had been in Poland. They were more accepted by their non-Jewish countrymen and, accordingly, had more liberty and better educational opportunities.

In October, 1943, news spread through the camp like a hurricane: the Totenkopf (death's head) S.S. was arriving to take over from the Schutzpolizei. Blechhammer was to complete its transition to becoming a concentration camp, Auschwitz was coming to us. It was being classed as a subcamp of Auschwitz with its name changed to Auschwitz III.

An S.S. Sturmbahnfuehrer was in charge. He was a mean-looking man, missing the index finger of his right hand, one of a series of cruel animals who began to blend in appearance into an incarnation, a symbol, of evil. The major had a staff of guards specially trained for death camp duty. This commandant, these guards, had no shard of sympathy in their beings. Their faces were set into rigid lines. Their identities were dominated by the twisted cross, which they each wore, and by the death's head—the skull—which looked sightlessly outward from their hats. We could expect no mercy. The goodness in these human beings had been so totally suppressed that it had ceased to exist. The beast dominated. Comparatively, what we had experienced before was a picnic.

The S.S. regarded Jews as subhumans: we had no right to live except that some of us might be needed as slaves for the Aryan masters and the German war effort. Jews were to be used as long as they were useful and then disposed of, like squeezing a lemon for its juice and throwing away the rind. Nazi policy was to make Europe Jew-free, so Jewish blood became very cheap. We were worked to exhaustion, then transported and gassed.

New rules were issued. There was more work, harder work, more discipline. Deviation was routinely punished by death, not just whippings, which might or might not lead to death.

We were all tattooed with numbers on our left forearms. This was done by prisoners brought from Auschwitz, working under close S.S. supervision. We each received a shirt, blue-and-gray striped pajamas and a matching round *chapo*. All of our civilian clothes and any valuables—watches, money, and so forth—which we had managed to keep with us had to be delivered to a collection point in camp, under penalty of death. Sadly, I placed my plywood case on that pile, finally stripped of all physical remnants of my past. We were each given a steel plate, cup, and spoon, with which to eat our rations, which were now handed out each evening at each barrack after assembly was called by a block elder. These utensils and our new clothes became our only possessions. Each item was marked with the same number as our forearm.

In addition to our number, our pajamas were marked with triangles colored to distinguish our offenses against Hitler's sensibilities. A red triangle designated a political prisoner, yellow a Jew, green a criminal, black a homosexual. Most of us were red or yellow.

The Sturmbahnfuehrer ordered a band organized from among the prisoners to provide martial music as we entered and left camp. After the morning assembly, the musicians stood at the gate, playing to march us off to work. Everything was done with military precision and rigor. During the day, the band members practiced under their S.S. supervisor or labored inside the camp. They had better rations than most of us and more freedom to move around within the compound.

When we returned to camp in the evening, we were greeted with music. Otherwise, our returning routine was much as it had been before the S.S. took over. The one difference was that sometimes we were searched as we marched in and anyone carrying anything but his clothes was mercilessly beaten. Indeed, we were kicked and beaten at the slightest whim of a guard. It was normal for inmates to have bruises, broken bones, and missing teeth. Possession of any kind of food, letters or newspapers was punishable by death. Death, indeed, became one of the commonest commodites in camp. The S.S. planted German, Polish, and a few Russian non-Jews in camp as informers. Often, we couldn't pinpoint who these men were, but when we spotted one we avoided him as best we could, since we knew they did their jobs well.

A system of bonus cards was instituted to reward those non-Jews—foremen and capos—who worked above the call of duty. A whorehouse was established using the Jewish women, but only Aryan prisoners could use their bonus cards there. A one-oven crematorium was built to dispose of "casualties."

A *Krankenbau* (hospital) was established in a separate barrack under the supervision of a half-Jew from Warsaw, with two "medics" as helpers. The supervisor was a real doctor. One of the medics had been a carpenter at home, the other a tailor. Casualties mounted daily, and the line seeking help never ended. Every so often, an S.S. doctor came from Auschwitz with a truck to pick up all those in the hospital who were unable to work and unlikely to be cured in a day or two, and transported them to the gas chamber.

The winter of 1943 was harsh, and we worked outside in bitter cold with inadequate clothing. Some prisoners covered their bodies with paper cement bags, trying to keep warm, but if they were caught they were as good as dead. Some of us suffered from frostbite. Those severely afflicted were treated at the hospital. If limbs, toes, or fingers had to be removed, their destinies were sealed.

The deprivation and hard work caused exhaustion. Workers became so tired they couldn't walk back to camp. They had to be carried, arriving half-dead, to be finished off by the S.S. and cremated in our new oven. They couldn't be left at the construction site to die in relative peace or to spare their bearers the extra strain because everyone had to be accounted for on the camp's balance sheet. If 5,000 bodies walked out to work, 5,000 must return, one way or another.

Among the punishments meted out, often for slight deviations, was the *"Straf Kommando,"* where the offender was made to carry heavy stones barefoot. Whenever someone sank under his burden, he was kicked and bludgeoned. Few survived the ordeal. At each day's end, ten or more often lay dead.

There was quite a rivalry among the S.S. men to see who could do the best job, who could be most cruel to the Jews and, perhaps, get a promotion.

There was one S.S. man who stood out in this competition. He wore his gun low and walked with the gait of a horseman. We nicknamed him Tom Mix. He carried a bullwhip always ready and did not need any reason to let it bite.

The S.S. men were not only good Nazis, but fierce anti-Semites. Their excuse for beating up Jews was *"Ihr habt den Christus ermorded"* (you murdered Christ—and for this you must suffer).

Every so often, a commission headed by an S.S. doctor arrived for "selection." We came to know this routine well. An assembly was called. Everybody had to stand outside in the cold for hours, half-naked, while the commission members selected the unfit. The S.S. asked those chosen for their numbers and doublechecked them with the tattoos on their forearms. Those called were taken away to death. I always rubbed my cheeks for ten to twenty minutes so they would look red and healthy. I must say I was lucky not to be selected because there was no meat left on my body. Every bone could be counted.

One day in Spring, 1944, two of my fellow-prisoners decided to escape and disappeared from the factory area. When their absence was discovered during the head count in the evening, the rest of us were marched back to camp where we stood until the next morning. Then we were marched back to work without sleep or food. That day, the two escapees were caught and brought back to camp. An assembly was called, and they were hanged before us in the name of S.S. Reichsfuehrer and Polizeifuehrer Himmler. After this lesson, falling over with exhaustion, we were dismissed.

Life was one hell on earth, but we got used to living in hell. There was no alternative but death. Even through this suffering, I wasn't willing to give up, preferring to hold on and fight no matter what. The prize was my very life.

In June, we began to hear news that raised our morale: the Americans had landed in Europe. On the eastern front, the German army was on the run. Towns like Lvov, Pinsk, and Tarnopol had been recaptured by the Red Army.

In July, we heard of an attempt to kill Hitler. Although it failed, we took it as a sign the German hierarchy was cracking up.

The war news became more glorious. We smuggled in pieces of newspapers we found in the construction area, carrying them into camp unless we saw it was a search night, in which case the scraps were eaten. Even the *Volkischer Beobachter,* the prime Nazi paper, couldn't hide the facts of the coming defeat.

The bombing of the factory intensified. A raid would shut down the power station. It would be repaired and fired up again, but, whenever its smoking chimney showed it to be back in operation, it was like a signal to the U.S.A.F., and long-range bombers appeared overhead by the hundreds to put out that fire again. It generally took two to three weeks each time to repair the damage and bring the factory back into production.

The R.A.F. heightened the pressure on the Germans, visiting us frequently to drop time bombs. My fellow inmates were the chosen people to dig them up so the German Engineer Corps could defuse them. Quite a few of us were blown up by the bombs. Those lucky enough to survive got an extra bowl of soup, an incentive sufficient to attract volunteers.

Air-raid shelters—ditches about seven feet deep, covered

with railroad ties or trees and mounded with six to eight feet of dirt—zig-zagged through the area. Each held 200 people. Naturally, the Germans had first claim on them. On occasion, we were chased outside to be exposed to bombs and shrapnel, and many of our people were unwittingly killed by the Allies, for whom we wished victory.

One day in August, the chimney was again smoking, so we were expecting an air raid. The attacks generally came between 11:00 and 11:30 A.M., so we prepared ourselves, as did the Germans. This time, however, the U.S.A.F. was early. Panic struck when the sirens began their miserable howl, a sound I could not stand then and have hated since, because it reminds me of death and destruction. That day, it also reminded me that people somewhere cared and were fighting Hitler's evil with all their might.

The planes came in so low you could see the pilots. Bombs fell indiscriminately as we ran to an air-raid shelter. About fifty of us laborers ducked into a shelter, but we were not destined to stay there long. Just as we settled down, an S.S. guard shouting, *"Alle Juden raus, heraus schnell"* (all Jews out, out quickly!), came in. This order, no empty threat, was given at gunpoint. We had no choice but to obey. We ran in all directions, looking for another shelter, never looking back. Bombs fell all around us. A couple of us found a crater left from an earlier raid and jumped in, throwing ourselves flat to lie shivering and trembling in fear.

Bombs fell near us, and we were covered with dirt. I touched my body to see if everything was where it belonged. As the bombs slowed and the sound of the planes faded, I stood up and looked around. The shelter we had been chased from had taken a direct hit. I heard crying and yelling from the rubble that remained of it. One hundred Germans were dead and about an equal number injured. We had the task of digging out the victims and carrying them to the factory clinic. For a long time, I had been at odds with my God, but that day I said a silent prayer of thanks.

In the aftermath of the attack, a few of my campmates decided to escape. The commotion of the moment hid their departure, but their absence was quickly noticed as we marched back into camp. The rest of us were kept assembled, at attention, while the guards searched for them. They were found in the middle of the night, brought back to camp and hanged publicly. It was 3:00 A.M. before we were allowed to sleep. Three hours later, we were marched out to work, everybody, once more, falling down in exhaustion.

During lunch hour, I found a quiet corner to rest in. I couldn't stay awake. My next memory was of being awakened by a German foreman, who wrote down my number. I had slept into the work shift. My nap qualified, under camp rules, as sabotage. I was frightened and uncertain, not knowing what my destiny would be. If the German reported me, it was my end. But, perhaps, he had a heart and wouldn't report me. Three weeks went by and nothing happened, though I spent many sleepless nights worrying.

Then, on Yom Kippur, the Day of Atonement, the holiest of holy days in the Jewish faith, we were marched into camp through a different gate from usual. I knew something was cooking. We were confronted by a platform, on which were four gallows, for victims yet unknown. We didn't have to wait long to find out who they were. The guards called out numbers. I steeled myself to be included, remembering the German who had taken my number at work. The first three were not mine. The fourth began: "1 . . . 7 . . . 8 . . . 2. . . ." I fainted.

Two of my companions brought me to. Fortunately, we were toward the back of the assembled mass of prisoners, and my collapse had not been noticed by the guards.

"What happened?" I asked, a question they echoed.

I had blacked out on hearing the first four digits of my number—178246. However, they told me the number called had ended in different digits and belonged to a young Dutch Jew, whose face I'll never forget as long as I live.

The four called had been found examining yellow powder from an unexploded bomb by an S.S. man who reported them to his superiors. For that "crime" they were meeting the hangman.

The Germans proceeded with their ceremony: "In the name

of Reichsfuehrer and Polizeifuehrer of the S.S., these four are found guilty of sabotage and hereby convicted to death by hanging," the guard announced.

They marched their victims onto the platforms, positioning them on wooden horses under the nooses, but before the rope was placed around his throat, the Dutch Jew, whose name I never found out, said, "Comrades, may you be lucky and be liberated and return to your homes."

The horses were pushed from under the victims, leaving them dangling, their faces turning blue as they slowly strangled. There was no neck-snapping sudden fall at this execution. As the four were hanged, the Dutch Jew's rope tore, and he fell to the ground, living. There was a sigh of relief from our assembly. We prayed that, perhaps, his life would now be spared, but that wasn't about to happen. Tom Mix climbed up with a new rope and tested its strength, and the Dutch Jew was hanged again, this time for good. May God rest his soul.

We were dismissed and sent to go about our limited business as if nothing had happened. I touched myself to verify that I was still in one piece, saying to myself, "You lucky son of a gun."

As the days passed, the military experts in our group busily interpreted the news we gathered from various sources, including the scraps of newspapers that managed to get into camp without being eaten.

We had among us a man who had been a major in the German Imperial Army during World War I. He was a tall, distinguished-looking man in his late forties, a German Jew, who maintained a military bearing and had demonstrated a fierce drive to live. He had worn his medals and ribbons, earned for distinguished bravery, with great pride. One day, shortly after the S.S. had taken over, a young guard had come up to him and asked him how much coffee he had paid for the medals and ripped them from his lapel. When the major protested, he was slapped across the face again and again, and he burst into tears, like a little child, when the guard left with his ribbons. While he continued to follow the war news, and occasionally still joined in analysis, his interest had become halfhearted. His morale was broken, and with it his will to live. Within a few months, this broken man was dead.

In the news that filtered through to us was word that Paris had been liberated by the French Free Forces. The French Jewish inmates were ecstatic: their home was liberated and, perhaps, they, too, would soon be free and able to return there.

How far away could the end be, we thought. The German effort was being repelled on all fronts, with Hitler's troops retreating everywhere. The U.S. Army was driving for the Rhine River, bringing the war to Germany. In the East, the Red Army reached the Wista River near Warsaw. The Poles took up weapons and fought the Germans in the streets of the city. Strangely, the Red Army paused when it crossed the river. Its leaders could see the fighting with field glasses and yet they waited until the Germans had destroyed Warsaw and herded the Polish fighters off to concentration camps before they advanced.

Maybe the civilized world could yet smash into the heart of Nazi Europe, we thought, and before our lives were lost.

On the day we heard of the liberation of Paris, we received with our daily rations for the first time two square pieces of soap imprinted "R.J.F." Word went around that the initials meant *"Reines Juedishes Fett"* (pure Jewish fat). We joked in the wash barracks: "You are washing yourself with your father; you are washing with your mother." Weeks later, we found out the joke was on us. The Germans didn't waste anything. They gathered the fat from the gassed corpses and made soap out of it to distribute to the inmates of concentration camps. Until we discovered this, we had washed ourselves with our loved ones. After that, we stopped bathing with soap.

As the allies advanced, our rations were cut and cut again. Where a loaf of hard dark bread had been divided among four inmates, it now became food for six. Inmates who were not ablebodied were being transported weekly to Auschwitz. Selection became more common, and each time I rubbed my cheeks to healthy redness, almost making my face bleed.

One cloudy Monday, during lunch break, I was given a sandwich by the German corporal for whom I had worked since returning from Sagan. Tom Mix passed by and caught me eating it. I jumped to attention, almost choking on a piece of bread. He asked me where and from whom I got the sandwich. I told him I had found it on the floor. He did not believe me. He broke a leg from a chair and asked again where I got the sandwich. No matter the consequences, I just couldn't tell him the truth. I was in trouble already, and the truth would not have helped me. I told him again that I found it on the floor. He swung the wooden chair leg at me. I ducked. He got mad, ordered me to stay at attention and knocked out a couple of my teeth. These, luckily, only came from one side of my mouth. He began to hit me all over, but I stuck to my story. I still carry scars from that beating, but I was lucky to escape that easily from an encounter with the meanest S.S. guard in the camp. I was shaken but my wounds healed in a couple of weeks.

My life could have been much worse. I had an easier job than most of my fellow-inmates. My corporal was grateful that I hadn't broken under the severe beating and given him away, and from then on, I was even more alert to avoid Tom Mix whenever possible than I had been.

Meanwhile, the band played on. In addition to its daily marches, it had to perform for the S.S. guards on Sundays. It put on a good show. Among the musicians was an Austrian Jew named "Chatckes," a virtuoso—a magician—with the fiddle. Singers would join the band for its weekend concert, as would several inmates who literally were magicians and did all kinds of tricks to amuse our tormentors. The singers were excellent, with such fine voices and ability to sing Jewish songs that even the S.S. liked them.

During that summer, the Dutch Jews in camp had a quiet celebration. I wasn't sure if it was for their queen's birthday or for the birth of a new princess. Whichever it was, I have never seen so much love for a country or monarch, especially considering the circumstances. I envied them. Most of us had nothing to celebrate, nobody to cheer. The few Jews who were lucky enough to escape into the forests and become partisans were hunted by the Germans and also by their Polish comrades in the so-called "Home Army" or "Armia Krajowa."

Camp was shaken daily by shootings, beatings, torture. The guards, and especially the commandant, became nervous because of the news from the fronts. They must have realized they were fighting a losing war, and they took this out on us.

Trucks heading from other camps passed through Blechhammer ever more frequently. Occasionally, I recognized a girl from Bendin, a task that required seeing past the living skeletons they had become to see the young women of my memory. All you could see of them as they were carted through were faces and desperate eyes. All we could feel was sorrow. We already knew their next destination: the gas chamber at Auschwitz.

Among the women in camp, I made the acquaintance of a girl named Mary, who had come from a town near Bendin. We became friends for some reason. Maybe it is a woman's instinct or desire to care for someone. In any event, Mary, who was in charge of laundry in the wash barrack, gave me extra clean shirts and underwear. She seemed happy just to talk to me for a minute or two and not be caught, and I was happy to be able to keep myself clean; it made me feel better. Each day, after the evening assembly, I always managed to stop in the shoe-repair shop where Mary would wait to ask me how the day had been. It was nice to have a friend among such a surfeit of enemies.

In November, I became sick. I awoke one morning and found I had trouble lifing my left arm. I examined myself and discovered an ulcer under the arm. Just thinking that I might have to go to the clinic made me even sicker. I decided to go to work and hope I would be all right. I could get some help at work, I knew, to cut down the strain of the job, but I hoped I wouldn't need help for long. Even the friendliest German could cover up for me only for a short time. However, I grew worse during the day and had a fever by the time we returned to camp. My head was spinning. My temperature was 104. The sore under my arm throbbed constantly. Clearly, it was infected. I became desperate. As I staggered back into camp, I decided that whatever would be, would be. After roll call, I gathered my courage and went to the clinic. The line was half a mile long. After about an hour, I was called in and asked what was wrong. They knew I worked as an electrician, and, of everyone in camp, I was the last person they had expected to see. I undressed, raised my arm, and looked at the medic. I knew the sore was bad and had to be taken care of right away. So did he. Without saying anything to me, the medic, the one who had been a carpenter, turned my head away and made an incision with a regular kitchen knife; he didn't have any better instruments. He drained the wound and dipped a string of gauze in a yellow liquid he called "Rivanol." He put it deep into the incision. It hurt like hell, but there was no choice. I was brought before the doctor in charge. He was, and had for many years been, a practicing Christian, but was in camp because one of his parents had been Jewish. He was a pleasant, caring man but could do only so much with the limited facilities he was given. Initially, he gave me five days off work during which I had to stay in the sick bay to be accounted for while not going to roll calls.

Sick inmates did not receive even the full measure of the camp's starvation diet. Those in Krankenbau were served only a bowl of soup and a cup of muddy water, referred to as coffee. Mary, an angel of mercy, found out I was in sick bay and, risking severe punishment, came to visit me every day, bringing me bread and soup. Sometimes she even managed to get soup from the S.S. kitchen. She was a real lifesaver. After the war, I found out she was liberated in Bergen-Belsen by the British Eighth Army and sent to Sweden to recuperate.

There were two rooms used for sick bay, each with forty beds—twenty double bunks. I was assigned an upper bunk. All of the beds in my room were filled, most with victims of exhaustion and malnutrition.

After three days in there, my fever receded, but I still couldn't lift my arm properly. At about noon that day, our doctor came into the room accompanied by an S.S. doctor. The visitor walked through sick bay, pausing to ask about each patient's sickness. When he reached me he asked our doctor, "What's the matter with this boy?" The doctor answered that I had a minor ulcer and was to return to work the next day. He took thirty-nine charts from the room, leaving only mine. All of the others were picked up the next day to be trucked to Auschwitz and gassed.

I was kept in sick bay for another five days—eight in all—since the doctor told me he didn't expect another inspection until the next month. Fear made me anxious to go back to work, but the doctor reassured me each time I asked, insisting there would be no more danger and I should rest my arm as much as possible. When I finally left, I thanked him from the bottom of my heart. I could say I was born anew after gambling with death. I felt I was like a cat, with nine lives, which were being taken one at a time, but, at least for then, I knew they had not run out. When I was checked out of sick bay and returned to my regular barrack, I was assigned to my old job, and was glad to be back at the power station.

The weather became very cold, but, again, Mary was a lifesaver to me. She knit me a sweater, unraveling yarn from old sweaters she had saved from the laundry. I wore it under my regulation clothes so it was not visible to watching guards and informers. She also found some warm underwear for me.

The bombing became more and more intensive, from the Americans by day and the British by night. Quite a few prisoners were killed, since we were generally exposed to the falling bombs death, and if someone was wounded and incapable of working, his destiny was sealed; he was gone as if he had never existed.

We celebrated another Christmas, my fifth birthday in captivity. How many more would I celebrate so, I wondered.

The German war effort continued to falter. The Russians attacked on all eastern fronts and the other Allies fought on in the west, despite being stopped temporarily in Belgium in the Battle of the Bulge. We knew that eventually they would break through and drive the Germans back within their own borders. There was talk about Blechhammer being liquidated. We wondered what would become of us. We could hear fighting in the distance, especially the thunder of big guns. "Whose guns are those?" we asked among ourselves. "How far away are they? Are we going to be liberated by the Red Army? By the Western Allies? Would we, for that matter, ever be free again?"

We had only a few weeks to speculate. On January 21, we were told that all of us who were able to walk, must assemble and draw rations for three days. Since we had no things to pack, when we drew our rations we were ready to march to our unknown destination.

There were 5,000 of us. Only those who were in sick bay were left behind, in the hands of destiny. A few ablebodied prisoners hid under the barracks and thus escaped what we would come to call "The Bloody March." I considered this alternative but feared the S.S. would burn down the barracks as we left.

History records that my captivity would have been shorter had I hidden. The Russian armies under Marshal Konev liberated those who remained of Blechhammer's inmates a few days after we marched out. Those armies were to liberate Auschwitz, as well, on January 27, 1945.

Buchenwald

The Bloody March

We were marched into the bitter cold, clothed in our inadequate pajamas and useless pillbox hats. Our path lay through deep snow, with the guards pushing us to stay ahead of the Russians. Hunger, as well as the initial pain of overeating, dogged us. Most of the camp's inmates were so hungry that, having three day's rations in their hands—a whole loaf of bread—they ate it in one sitting, leaving themselves with nothing for later. A few of us managed to let our common sense dominate our abiding hunger and save our crumbs for what would come.

On the first day, we were marched about twenty miles under these most strenuous of conditions. The second day, things got rougher. Prisoners who fell behind were shot on the spot. A mass slaughter was in the making. We quickly learned to stay as much as possible in the center of the column of marchers. Neither end was safe, since periodically the guards would reverse the order of march; the front of the line would become the back, and a new group of instant stragglers became machine-gun fodder.

By the third day, hunger pains ate at all of us. Even the most cautious had used up his food. Snow was our only nourishment. Sleeping through the bitter winter nights in the snow added to the march's toll. Many went to sleep and never awoke.

On the fourth day, the S.S. obtained ten horse-drawn wagons from a nearby farm for those having trouble walking. At dusk, they took the wagons to the local cemetery and everyone in them was machine-gunned.

On the fifth day, hunger was so bad that many of my companions just lay down to be shot. They just couldn't make it. Sons left fathers behind and fathers left sons. They bewailed their fate silently, but could do nothing else. The only other choice was to lie down with the dying one and remain forever.

By day six, there were 800 fewer prisoners than had left Blechhammer. That evening, we arrived at a farm where the farmer boiled potatoes for us, but not enough for us all.

There was a run on the potatoes. The S.S. shot, and pieces of brain mixed with the food. I was sickened, though it is a mystery where my stomach found anything to vomit. I wouldn't eat the potatoes even if it meant starvation. I took some small pleasure in sleeping in a barn that night and taking off my shoes for the first time since we set out.

The next day, we were marched through a large town. The German people stood along the sidewalks on our route, laughing and spitting at us, the Jewish criminals. I can still hear their laughter. A short time later, they would be running for their lives; the Red Army paid them back in kind.

The eighth day I became sick, stricken with a bad case of diarrhea, my waste reddened by blood. My mind worked overtime seeking a cure. I hadn't come that far to give up. At last, I came up with an answer.

At our next stopover, another farm, I asked around for cocoa, which I knew from before the war would soothe my gut. Once locked up, we could circulate freely within our quarters. Despite the rules against possessions, many of us had hidden small caches of potential valuables in camp, which we had taped to our bodies or otherwise secreted on our persons when we vacated Blechhammer. There were prisoners who had worked with English prisoners of war at the factory and had gathered a supply of cocoa, trading services for goods. It had always been possible, though risky, to get around the guards.

I was desperate, asking everybody if he knew someone who had some. Finally, I found a fellow who had worked in the camp shoe-repair shop, who had a few ounces in a metal container. I offered him my last hundred marks, which I kept in case of emergency, and this was a case of greatest emergency. He accepted the money, though he probably felt he would never be able to use it. He was a goodhearted man.

I managed to contact the farmer, who gave me some hot water. I mixed the cocoa powder with it and drank. That night, I slept peacefully and in the morning felt better.

I felt that God was testing my faith. I prayed for the sick and the weary, asking for strength to endure and survive and to be worthy of being liberated and finding freedom. I could not understand how the atrocity I was living could be happening. We walked, leaving a trail of blood and bodies. By the time of my illness, we had lost 1,200 souls, people who had struggled on, hoping to survive. Their hope had been shattered and they lay dead, without even the solace of a decent burial. Wolves, hungry dogs, and other of nature's scavengers ate what was left of them.

At the end of the nine days it took us to reach our destination, the trail of bodies totaled 1,500. We reached the gates of Gross Rossen convinced, wrongly we would find out, that we had experienced the worst trials the fates had to offer.

It turned out that only one hundred days were left until the German Reich would crumble and we would be free, but those days would provide the fullest manifestation we had yet seen of Hell's evil on this earth.

K.Z. Gross Rossen

Our straggling mass of marchers was halted about 100 yards from the fences of our new home, and the guards formed us into proper military columns. As smartly as we could, we marched through Gross Rossen's gates, being counted as we entered, to join some 5,000 prisoners already in the concentration camp. Our S.S. guards were ordered, then and there, to the eastern front, leaving us to even more cruel caretakers. We were divided into two groups, each in front of a bare, new, cement-floored wooden barrack. We were put in the charge of capos, most of whom were Germans imprisoned for a variety of crimes. The capos' chairs were the only furniture in the barracks. The rest of us sat on the floor, crowded together like sardines.

Immediately, we were given a taste of what to expect from our new home. After counting the prisoners in front of the barrack, the capos took those weakened by fever, by frostbite, or just by unbearable circumstances, and placed them on the ground; which was mud to a depth of about two feet. Then they bashed in their heads using shovels. Through these were virtually mercy killings, they were motivated by greed for extra rations, not by any degree of compassion.

There were those among us who envied these dead. They had no more misery, no more suffering, no more hunger. I had a different idea. I resolved more strongly to live, to see the end of the beasts and of the dark age which the Nazis brought down on us.

You could see despair spread, however. The constant sight of electrified wire, which made all hope of escape impractical, and the deaths of our fellows day by day were to chip away at our sanity. Many of us, had we had the strength, would have run to the wires and ended our misery. Throughout each day, roll calls were called haphazardly to intimidate us and to weaken us by keeping us standing for hours. All the capos had to do was push someone into the mud to mark his end. He could not lift himself, nor could we help him.

Gross Rossen was an old camp which the Nazis had expanded to hold an influx of victims. The older, established barracks were on a hill; the newer, prefabricated structures we were put in were in a valley, which was quickly dubbed the "Valley of the Dead." At Gross Rossen there was no work. Even that minimum dignity of accomplishment that came from a ditch well dug, from another day meeting the challenge of surviving, was taken from us in the valley and exchanged for a mind-deadening, featureless passage of time spent vegetating in a minimal cramped space on the cold concrete floor of the barrack or in the clammy mud of the valley. There was little to break the monotony of our hours.

Some time was available to wander around the confines of the camp, looking into the faces of our companions, past the sameness of our striped pajamas and the ravages of our ordeal. You had to look deep into those faces to recognize someone.

A few days after our arrival, as I wandered the valley, I was confronted with an apparition. My heart stopped. He looked closely at me, even as I probed his face. I rubbed my eyes wondering if the man before me could indeed be my brother Jack, whom I hadn't seen in four years. He, too, hesitated. Then he fell into my arms and started crying. I just stood there holding him, overwhelmed but unable to return his tears. I had none left.

Jack, it turned out, was already an oldtimer at Gross Rossen, having arrived a few days before us with a group from camp Maslovitz. When he had heard that the inmates of Blechhammer had arrived, he began asking about me since he knew

I was interned there. We could move around in camp as we wished, though always at the risk of missing a roll call, and so he had searched for me.

Jack was housed on the hill, where roll calls were fewer and the barracks had some straw on the floor. After that morning's roll call, he had come down and asked around to see if anyone knew where I was, if I still lived. We met midway up the hill.

We recovered our composure and stood looking at each other. Still trembling with joy, Jack took from his shirt a little pouch of tobacco which he carried by his heart and handed it to me. Since there had just been a roll call, we felt we had time to talk. He took me up to his barrack, where we bribed the block elder with some of the tobacco so he would let me stay with Jack for the day. Jack also had a half-ration of bread. How he managed to carry that meager portion and not eat it right away was a mystery to me. He handed it to me, but I refused. He touched me as if to check that I was still in one piece and we began to tell each other our experiences of the past four years. He still shook from his excitement, his eyes filled with love as he looked me over.

Finally, he calmed down and began to fill me in on what had happened after I left home. He told me how Mother had been heartbroken, crying that she would never see her firstborn son again. Father said it was God's will, that God's wish marked our destiny. He had prayed that the Almighty would have mercy on us all.

But the reality.... Jack told me how scared they were when Freckle Face first visited our house in his S.A. uniform. All our neighbors had gone into hiding. How surprised they had been when he produced a letter, written in Jewish, from me. Jack told me how he had taken care of Freckle Face, searching out vodka for him, and how they had become used to his visits and, indeed, couldn't wait until he would come again.

He told me about Gertrude's visit, how beautiful she was, and how she tried to convince my parents that she could help me escape and hide me for the duration of the war.

Life in Bendin had become unbearable. The strongarm types had gained power, most becoming informers for the Germans or the local Jewish policemen. They were merciless. Survival at the expense of others became the practice. Jews in power blackmailed other Jews, the common means of trade being barter. The wealthy were those with hard currencies like dollars, British pounds, and Swiss francs, which were still accepted for goods.

Daily "requests" by the German authorities for more Jewish manpower became intolerable. People were caught in the streets and sent to destinations unknown. Sometimes it was better to "volunteer" for forced-labor camps.

Jack told me how Papa used to sit up late into the night filling factory-made cardboard and paper tubes with tobacco for me, motivated by his love.

He told me what he knew of our family's plight, of who was caught by the Germans and where they were, and of those who had disappeared as if they'd never existed.

I told him I had heard that Papa and our youngest brother, Sam, were in forced-labor camp Klettendorf near Breslau. We hoped they were all right. Perhaps they would pull through, since we could feel in our bones that the end was coming.

We talked for hours, discussing experiences during our separation. Then we parted, promising we would not be separated again if we could help it.

I walked back down into the valley, to my miserable quarters. In the barrack, my fellow inmates were sitting on the cement floor pressed together like sheep. The capo, a German wearing the green triangle of the criminal, a short, stocky man named Zimmerman, was dressed in red swimming trunks and carrying a shovel. He had a pair of helpers, one a Jew, the other also a German criminal, whose names I never found out. They carried spades. As night came, they went to work hitting the prisoners sitting in front of them over the head, breaking their skulls so they would collect their rations. By morning, twenty inmates lay dead on the floor. Life was cheap. Death was worth a hundred grams of dry bread, soaked with blood.

I couldn't sleep, keeping instead a watchful eye on Zimmerman. I tried to stay in the middle of the pack to avoid being hit or crushed by the pressure of the other inmates pushing away from our tormentors toward the walls.

In the morning, we stood at attention for roll call. We were counted in front of our barracks. The living, added to the corpses now piled at the barrack's entrance accounted for everyone. The S.S. left until the next roll call. Of the 5,000 who left Blechhammer, about 2,750 still lived, and the number continued to shrink.

As soon as we were dismissed, I ran to Jack's barrack and told him about what had happened in the night. He begged me to be alert and very careful from then on. We talked some more about the past, until my exhaustion caught up with me and I fell sound asleep with Jack watching over me as if I were a helpless babe.

I woke in time for the next roll call. A few shoves and pushes had again resulted in casualties: men dead in the mud from beating and exhaustion. In the evening, after yet another roll call, Zimmerman and his henchmen went back to the work they knew best. I was sick to my stomach. We were at their mercy. The casualties among those sitting on the floor mounted. As the capos killed, the inmates in front moved back, so those by the wall were crushed by the weight of human bodies, as if an avalanche had hit them. I continued to seek the middle of the mob as much as possible. Day in, day out, for the seventeen days we were in that hole, the hideous routine went on. I began to doubt if any of us would ever walk out of that godforsaken camp, which we called Hell!

The fight for survival was on, with skirmishes constantly, every hour, every minute, every second. I spent the daylight hours between roll calls with Jack in his barrack. Evenings, I went back to the "kingdom," where the death watch continued and the toll mounted, tallied outside the barrack at each morning roll call. The ritual of disposing of the dead followed each morning roll call. Each day, more prisoners reached the camp from other parts of the crumbling Reich. Each day more were shipped on to other camps in a continuing shuffle that taxed and diminished those prisoners, Jewish and otherwise, who still fought for life.

The Red Army had reached German soil, and we expected that Gross Rossen would be closed and we moved again at any hour. We were very much afraid that, in an attempt to cover up its atrocities, the S.S. would kill us all, perhaps with machine guns, perhaps by other means. We were in the dark, cut off at that time from any news from the outside world.

Then, one day we were told to get ready for transport. We didn't know where we were heading, but I, for one, was glad to be leaving the godforsaken confines of Gross Rossen. My main concern was to avoid being separated from Jack again.

I felt contempt for the Nazis. I wished to be a soldier again and die fighting with a rifle in my hand, with dignity. An outsider would shake his head in disbelief at tales of the Nazi attrocities, but I was there. I saw starvation, maimings, and mass killings. It was no longer just the Jews who were to die. All prisoners from all over Europe were being killed. There were as many non-Jews among us as Jews.

On my last night in Gross Rossen, the killing was accelerated. Perhaps Zimmerman thought an occasion like this would never recur, and so he and his helpers let loose all restraint and killed and killed until they were too tired to swing their shovels. By morning, the toll of dead in our barracks exceeded fifty.

That morning, all block elders and capos were called to the main gate by the S.S. guards. When they returned, we were told to pack up and fall out in rows of three. Not everyone was to go. Zimmerman, for example, remained behind. I worried about Jack. Pandemonium broke loose. "On your feet," the capo's were yelling. "Everybody out of the barrack. Queue up. On your feet, you pigs. Line up by threes."

We were marched to the main gates, where 3,000 of us were counted and recounted for transport.

For the first time since our arrival, the commandant, a *Sturmbahnfuehrer* from Totenkopf S.S., appeared before us, swaggering along, swinging his bullwhip and quite a few obscenities in our direction. He said that if we thought we had it bad under him, we were in for a big surprise. We were to be shipped to Buchenwald.

Fear chilled my body. This was like taking shelter from the rain under a waterfall.

"As you walk out the gate, you'll get rations for three days, and, if the transport takes eight or ten days, you might as well die on the train," he said.

The breakdown of human decency, more than hunger, thirst, crowding, and lack of sleep, more than the outbreak of squabbles or the fear of what lay ahead, dominated the start of our journey. We drew our meager ration. Some of us couldn't wait even a second and started consuming the bread at once. I cut mine into six pieces and put it inside my shirt, close to my heart. I noticed Jack in line to draw his ration and was pleased that we were going to be together. We moved together. Our group formed three columns of twenty people for each cattle wagon or open coal car provided to carry us. We were ordered to march out of camp.

As we moved, we passed the women's camp. Inside we noticed our cousin Fay, whose mother had spent those last months rooming with our mother in Bendin. We got her attention, and she appeared to recognize us. She waved goodbye. We waved back. We were never to see her again.

The S.S. marched us about 500 yards to the railway station. The train consisted of fifty-two cars, twenty of them open. It was February 13, still winter, still cold. Our group was assigned an open car. In addition to the cars for the prisoners, there was a passenger car behind the locomotive and a caboose. In these, the guards rode. We were loaded, and, after waiting for a couple of hours, we started to the next stop in our odyssey. Except for the cold, things were worse in the closed wagons than the open. In each of the inmates' cars, there were two empty pails to serve as toilets, one on each side, and one pail of fresh water. In the open cars, at least, we had fresh air and could look at the sky. We could stand by the outside boards and relieve ourselves without fighting through the press of bodies to a bucket. Those closed in had to deal with the stink of the pails of their companions. The sick, the weak, the old, those helpless to reach the pails through the jam eliminated their meager wastes where they sat, adding to the choking stench that filled those cars.

Jack and I huddled together for warmth. We rubbed each other's hands. We stood up in turns to move our feet.

At the train's first stop, the guards issued blankets to the open cars. Perhaps this unexpected kindness was prompted by a flicker of humanitarianism sparked by visions of the war's end. Regardless of motive, they threw sixty blankets into our car, which we distributed among ourselves and things began to look up. We developed some hope that we would survive this journey. We began to speculate about what to expect in Buchenwald, a camp famous for cruelty. We visualized tortures and deprivation, but it hardly seemed possible that it could be worse than Gross Rossen.

We also speculated about our chances of surviving until the war ended. We knew the German army was on the run along the entire eastern front. We also knew the Allied forces were approaching Germany from the west and that the German economy was a shambles with whole cities bombed out and in ruins. What we didn't know was how soon the Allies would reach us and how long we would be allowed to live.

By February 15, the third day on the train, many of our companions no longer had even a crumb left to eat and were consuming only water. Jack had taken charge of our bread, cutting it into smaller pieces than I had and rationing it so it would last for eight days. He could control his hunger better than I could control mine. That day we passed through Dresden. It was shortly after that once-beautiful city had been the target of the major air raid that reduced it to rubble and killed some 50,000 Germans. The town was still smoldering. Smoke choked the air. Here and there, a fire burned. From our open cars, we could see the damage done by the Allies, the ruin and the disarray.

Our train was stopped. The buckets were emptied and fresh water put aboard. The dead were taken off the cars, counted, and disposed of in some manner. Each wagon contributed a couple of bodies, victims of hunger and exhaustion. Red Cross nurses saw the train sitting there and approached, wanting to give us some hot soup, but our guards chased them away, saying, "Those are only Jews."

After about two hours, the train moved on, past more ruins. Chaos ruled. Seeing the disarray and watching myriad German refugees leaving their bombed-out city bolstered our hopes for survival.

We continued across Germany. Three more days went by. The train stopped periodically. At each stop, the dead and dying were taken off the transport. Those on their last breath got a bullet of mercy from our guards.

We arrived at Weimar, near Buchenwald, at midday. Fifty-four of us remained in our open car. As the train pulled in, the sound of airplanes grew in the air. They dived at our train, and bombs began to fall around us. The Royal Air Force was directing its precision bombing at our moving train. The pilots of the 200 or so English Lancasters didn't know if the contents of the train were military or not. The S.S. guards ran for cover. Those of us in the open cars who could, jumped off and sought shelter near the train. Those in the closed cars couldn't do anything about their plight. The bombardment lasted about fifteen minutes; to us it seemed an eternity.

After the planes left, the guards herded us together and took count. There were 500 casualties among the prisoners and ten guards killed. We were put back on the train and waited to continue, but it turned out our waiting would last three more days. The bombing had damaged the water main leading to the camp and we would not be permitted in because we couldn't be *"entlausd"* (disinfected) in the wash barracks, which were out of commission.

We lived on water alone ten kilometers from the gates of Buchenwald. The death toll on the train continued to mount. When we were finally allowed into the death camp on February

21, only forty were left on our car. The train was emptied, and the 2,000 prisoners who disembarked were counted and taken en masse to the wash barracks for hot showers. We were ordered to undress and leave all our belongings on one side of the showers. On the other side we were to receive new clothing. Any valuables that had been smuggled that far were taken away. The guards made thorough body searches. Then, in groups of twenty, we were marched into the showers. The feeling of hot water streaming down my body was indescribable.

We left the shower area and were marched to the next room, which contained two immense kettles filled with a Lysol-like disinfectant. Two prisoners—Russians or Ukrainians—held brooms made of birch branches with the leaves still on them, bound with wire. We had to lift both arms so we could be brushed with disinfectant in our armpits and crotches. When someone wasn't quick enough, he also got a slap or two in the face with the burning liquid.

The disinfecting process and many of the routine functions of the camp were controlled by a group of prison oldtimers, often men who had been incarcerated before the war. They were somewhat more humane than the Germans and administered a crude justice to the most cruel among the leaders of the incoming prisoners. If someone was pointed out by his companions as a capo or block elder who hadn't behaved humanely, his head was dipped into a kettle of Lysol for as long as it took him to collapse. There was no ceremony; nobody bothered with another corpse since corpses were wherever you turned. Five or six of our group died in that way.

In the next room, we were handed clothes. I received clean striped pajamas, a clean shirt, a new round striped hat, a pair of socks, and linen shoes with wooden undersoles. This was something new to me, the first time in my life I wore wooden shoes. Jack was right behind me. He got leather shoes, but they were ready to fall apart.

There were a few exceptions to the no-possessions rule. One was barbers, who were permitted to keep the tools of their trade and to cut the hair of their fellow inmates. Malnutrition kept hair growth slow, but what was there was kept short to discourage nesting vermin.

Outside again, we were formed into a column and marched to our quarters.

Buchenwald consisted of two sections. On higher ground, stood the old camp to which had been sent the early enemies of Hitler's rise to power. It consisted of stone barracks with double bunks. Twenty men were assigned to each room, each with a straw-filled sack for a pillow and two military covers. It held deserters and traitors as well as all manner of political prisoners. It had been built to hold about 5,000 prisoners but now contained twice that number. We called it the "big camp."

The new portion of camp, dubbed the "little camp," was separated from the old by barbed wire and consisted of more of the prefabricated type of wooden barracks that had been my homes for so many months. To these barracks came the prisoners of the war, the objects of Hitler's desire to "cleanse" the face of Europe. We slept in long wooden boxes, stacked in tiers of three and separated by boards. There were fifteen inmates assigned to each box. We were so cramped that we could only sleep on our sides, all in the same direction. When one of us turned during the night, all fifteen of us had to turn. My only consolation was that I was with my brother.

The camp was so crowded that even death did not clear berths quickly enough to make room for everyone being transported there. As new prisoners arrived, others had to be formed into transports to be shuttled to yet another camp. It was only a matter of time before we would be shipped out again.

After the evening roll call, we received a meager portion of bread and hot water masquerading as soup. At least, after nine days on the train in the cold, we could warm our guts.

The only work available to any of us who were still able to work was cleaning up the rubble from bombed-out buildings in Weimar. Weimar, the city of Goethe, the cradle of the ill-fated experiment in democracy that was the Weimar Republic, was shattered.

At 6:00 A.M., on my first full day in Buchenwald, roll was

called. I climbed out of my box to see a horrible scene. At each barrack entrance were piled the corpses gathered during the night. They were yellow, the skin stretched tautly over the bones, skeletons in parchment. Many were naked, stripped by other inmates who were so cold they wanted to wear double pajamas or exchange their shoes for others in better condition.

I looked around at people walking around listlessly, as if in another world, talking to themselves. Some just stared into the distance, seeing nothing around themselves.

The corpses mounted each morning, into the thousands. It made me constantly sick to my stomach. During my five to six weeks in Buchenwald, 20,000 people must have died through all manner of murder and deprivation.

The commandant and his infamous wife, Ilse Koch, the Bitch of Buchenwald, lived outside the camp perimeter. All administrative work was done by oldtime inmates who were Communists, Socialists, or other enemies of the Reich before the war. The guards came into the camp only for roll calls, to beat and punish prisoners, and to see to it that the dead were removed and cremated—stacked on pyres and soaked with gasoline—or buried in mass graves by bulldozers.

Since our arrival, I had been thinking about the big camp, seeking after a way to move there. By my third day, I decided that whatever would be, I had to try to change quarters to the old camp.

About midday on February 25, I knocked at the door of the camp administrative offices. I was told to enter and asked what I wanted. I hesitated. I knew that my life depended on convincing this man that I should be moved. I told him that I had been a member of the outlawed Communist party in Silesia. I said I had been in prison before the war broke out and had only been released when the guards had fled from the oncoming Russian army. I didn't know if this story would work but I had nothing to lose. My life was already nearly forfeit.

I was told to come back the next day for an answer.

After leaving the office, I ran to Jack to share my scheme with him. He couldn't believe it. I told him that being moved in with the prominent prisoners of the big camp, who still received packages from home, would help us both. Jack had reservations about the whole thing. He was afraid of being separated again. I told him not to worry, that everything would work out for the best.

I didn't sleep that night, thinking of being in a bed by myself. Even being on a straw sack would be better than being boxed in with fourteen other inmates and by morning finding that those sleeping next to you would never wake up again. Sometimes, you would find a dead man on each side of you. We breathed in the midst of death.

Everywhere were the dead and half-dead, and prisoners walking around as though entranced.

I woke early the next day, walked over to the wash barrack, undressed, and washed myself thoroughly. I felt better, returning for roll call and "coffee." I talked with Jack for a while and, about 10:00 A.M., I kissed and hugged him. He had tears in his eyes as he wished me good luck and I went to the administrative building, where I was told to wait. I sat nervously, but, fortunately, I didn't have to squirm too long. When I was called, I entered the office, took off my round hat, and stood at attention, awaiting the outcome of my plea. I was asked some questions, which were irrelevant, but when I said I had been in the camps since October, 1940, this seemed to make the difference. I was told to move into the old camp, into a stone barrack, and to report to the block elder, who would have been notified of my arrival. I couldn't believe what I was hearing. I was still standing at attention when I was told to go right away so I would not miss the lunchtime soup, which we in the little camp never received. I took off as if on wings. Again, somebody was watching over me!

When I arrived, the block elder assigned me to an upper berth, with its straw sack and two military blankets, one on the sack as a sheet and the other to be used as a cover. I was told the German whose berth I now occupied, a political prisoner, had been taken out the night before and shot. He had been part of Admiral Canaris's Abwehr, the counterintelligence arm of the government.

In the big camp, there were prominent people—high-ranking prisoners-of-war, priests, politicians, and other people of stature. I met Leon Blum, the former Prime Minister of France. The inmates in the old camp had the privilege of listening to radio, even though only German stations were permitted. This was piped into the barracks on an intercom. They could receive packages, whether from relatives who lived in Germany or through the Red Cross in Geneva. These contained goodies I hadn't seen since the war broke out.

Since I was getting soup twice daily, I could spare half my bread ration for Jack. I also picked up cigarette butts and gave the tobacco to Jack, who traded it for more food.

In the little camp, there were no medical supplies. Some prisoners had no shoes and went around barefoot. Food was meager and of poor quality. You couldn't enter the barracks without being attacked by fleas and other insects. Prisoners developed large boils all over their bodies. Sanitary conditions were atrocious. The water supply was shut off periodically, sometimes as punishment and sometimes by the bombing, which came with regularity.

In both camps, the prisoners were awakened in the middle of the night by S.S. guards with dogs. Some were chased outside naked and barefoot. It was just the beginning of March, and at night, the temperature still fell 20 to 25 degrees below freezing. We were kept outside in the bitter cold for an hour or more at a time. When the guards were out of earshot, my fellow-inmates complained that there couldn't be anything worse on earth. I said that as long as we breathed, we had hope and shouldn't give up. We had come a long way. "We can see the end near. Hang on," I said, while silently crying for those who couldn't hang on any longer. They fell in front of me, in back of me, and on both sides. By the time we would be dismissed after these nocturnal ordeals, there were always a few hundred new victims.

Human skins were collected by those in charge of the camp. Several prisoners were killed merely for the tattoos on their bodies. From their skins, Frau Ilse Koch made lampshades of all sizes and shapes. These victims were killed by injection, so their skins would be undamaged. The skins were removed and the tattooed areas dried out and made into shades or mounted and framed for household decoration.

In the big camp, we could listen to the news from O.K.W., "Oberkomando Der Wehrmacht." The Germans were retreating on all fronts. The Russians were only fifty miles from Berlin. We could expect to be evacuated soon.

I helped Jack every day, however I could. When we got the news that the Allied forces had crossed the Rhine, we knew they would reach us soon, and the question was whether we would be able to hold on. Perhaps the Nazis would blow up the camps and their inmates to hide their criminal atrocities.

In March of 1945, Hitler, in the shadow of defeat, ordered his "Final Solution" accelerated. He ordered the murder of all the remaining Jews in the concentration camps before they could be liberated by the Allied forces. Himmler also saw the war lost, but he wanted the remaining Jews as a bargaining chip in negotiations with the Allies. He made sure Hitler's order never reached the camps.

The commandants from each camp sought to hang onto their domains, with their henchmen, in order to avoid fighting the Russians, whom they feared. They were cowards, heroic killers of innocent people, and that only when the whole state was behind them.

In Buchenwald's small camp, the stink of death was overwhelming. Naked corpses lay all around. Many of those still breathing, covered with lice, sat lifelessly, only a movement of the eyes signaling any remnant of consciousness.

Walking through the camp I heard a fellow-Jew recite in Hebrew, "Hear, O Israel, The Lord is Our God, the Lord is One...." It was more than a prayer; it was an act of faith coming before he gave out his final breath, for then this Jew lay down his head and died with God's name on his lips.

Sometimes I wondered if it was good to be among the "Chosen People" and I take the blame for all the ills of the Gentiles. Sometimes I wondered if I wouldn't have been better off to have been born of a Christian father and mother and so escaped a wealth of suffering. But if that had been, perhaps I would have been drafted by the Germans to oppress and, perhaps, kill. Which would I have preferred to be? A killer? Better to be with the oppressed.

One could learn many good things from the Germans. Not all of them were killers, but many were silent about the killings, and that made them at least as guilty as the murderers.

There came a Monday morning on which, it seemed, the sun did not want to rise. The sky was leaden, heavy with snow. I was in my barrack when the news came over the radio that the Americans had crossed the Rhine River and heavy fighting was taking place. That door to Germany stood open for the Allied forces. The entire Ruhr industrial area was vulnerable. The reports carried names of cities like Cologne, Bonn, and Frankfurt. We knew our stay at Buchenwald would only last a few more days, that we were perhaps only hours from being transported again.

As the time of transport grew nearer, I began to feel guilty about moving to the big camp and leaving Jack below. Even though we had both benefitted from the move, I feared that it had made it more likely that we would be separated again as groups were taken away from Buchenwald. I couldn't stop thinking that, after finding Jack after four years, I had chosen to be separated from him again. My conscience bothered me. I couldn't sleep and, when I did manage to doze fitfully, nightmares beset me. Despite this, I had a premonition that Jack and I would someday be free, though I couldn't visualize how that would come to pass.

The day after the Americans crossed the Rhine, I was awakened by a rush of movement. Guards were rushing about, their German shepherd dogs barking and snapping, waking prisoners and lining them up at their barracks. Half the inmates of Buchenwald were being evacuated. I wished I were with Jack but I prepared myself for the worst. Assembly was called and, after roll call, we were dismissed as usual. For a couple of hours I watched the activity around me, wondering what was happening below. Then the block elder came and told me that, since I had come up from the little camp, I had been picked for the next transport and was to report back below to the barrack that had been a theater, where entertainments had been offered for the guards before Buchenwald became an overcrowded concentration camp, and which was now the assembly point for prisoners being shipped away. Move quickly, he said, because the transportees were already assembled to pick up a couple of days' rations for the trip.

I moved toward the theater through a turmoil of bodies being prodded in all directions. Groups were being collected for various other camps, some to travel by foot, some by train.

The theater buzzed noisily, like a beehive. It was filled with people from all over Europe who had been united by a common suffering. I saw many men who had been lucky enough to survive the ordeals of death march and death camp, of bombings by the Allied air forces and of train rides through cold and starvation. All had shared the Gehenna of Buchenwald. There were more than 1,000 of us in the theater who were still deemed healthy enough to work and were destined for a camp near Schwarzwalde—the Black Forest—named Bissengen, where the Germans produced oil from shale. I pressed through the crowd asking after Jack. I became desperate. I called his name, becoming hoarse from the effort. Finally, I saw him in the rear of the room, and he saw me. He came to me with loving eyes and tender caring, and fell into my arms. My heart filled with joy, but I still could not find the tears to cry. The camps hardened their victims to steel, burning away softer emotions. We sat together to await the order to march out. I talked of the wonders of the big camp, he of all the miseries of the small. The most important thing was that we were alive, with no broken limbs. I trusted that together we could face the next unknown much better than we could separately.

We finally were called outside for roll call. There was the usual pushing and shoving, the final count, the *"Muetzen auf"* in front of the commandant, and then we left the infamous gates of Buchenwald.

K.Z. Bissingen

We carried meager rations for two days' traveling as we marched out. Some of us finished the rations before we reached the railway station. When we got to the train after an hour of exhausting marching, we were counted again and herded into closed cattle wagons in lots of sixty. In each car there were two buckets for natural uses and one of water for the two-day journey, which would last three days due to bombardment of rail lines by the Allied air forces.

The stench in the cars was unbearable. People who were lying on the floor, breathing only polluted air, gave up and died around us. Stronger ones made their way to a little window covered with iron bars to seek a whiff of air from outside. Our situation lost definition, becoming a blur of pain, which resolved itself only when we finally arrived at our destination. About 120 corpses of men who were just too weak to endure were carried off at the ride's end. The living were counted. So were the dead. The Germans remained meticulous to the end: *"Ordnung muss sein"* (There must be order).

Columns were formed. "Forward march," we were ordered, and off we went for another hour's march to the gates of another camp: Bissingen.

We were greeted with familiar words: an exhortation that we were there to work for the victory of Germany, that there was no way out except by death. "Onward to victory," even as fighting took place on German soil from the Rhine River in the west to the Oder in the east.

We were assigned barracks. The camp contained about 2,000 prisoners, many more than it had been built for. About 500 of us were crammed into a barrack designed to hold 300 prisoners. There were some bunks, but many of us slept on the straw-covered floor, disturbing the fleas and other vermin that lived there.

We were awakened the next morning and, after roll call, were marched to a work site where we broke up shale, loaded the shards into carts, and transported them to an open space where they were heated to force out the oil they contained. The heating area resembled a large broiler pan. The rocks were laid over pipes, which warmed them, and the oil ran down into runnels which carried it away for processing. As the stones gave up their treasure, we removed them and brought in fresh shale.

It was still cold out, and many of the prisoners gave in to the temptation to lie on the warm stones. However, the fumes rising from the hot oil made those who sought this comfort sick, and they often had to be carried from the stones into a field where they were allowed to recover, if they could.

We worked twelve-hour shifts, with many casualties daily. There was little rest in the barrack after work, either. A Hungarian Jew named Imri was block elder, and he was a bully who railroaded us beyond endurance.

Jack and I had somehow managed to be assigned as mechanics. We worked in a shop, fixing tools, so we weren't exposed to the cold too much.

After about seventeen days, we began to hear artillery fire not far from camp, and we knew we were going to be moved again. As the Allies advanced, we were constantly shuffled to stay ahead of them, and our tenure in each camp became shorter.

Sure enough, the day after we heard the guns, we did not go to work. After morning roll call, we were dismissed, only to be reassembled suddenly a short time later. We were lined up in four columns. Looking around, I discovered that I had been separated from Jack. I spotted him nearby and called him to join me so we would be together when we were marched out. For some reason, this time Jack refused to listen! This was odd, since I was the elder and he always had followed my instruction. I shrugged. This was no time to haggle. I wanted to be with him, and that day I was the one who had to move. I ran to his column, past the capos who stood monitoring us, suffering a blow on the head from a stick swung by a Jewish capo from Warsaw.

Bissingen was surrounded by natural beauty, which was breathtaking when there was time to enjoy it but which we had largely ignored under our circumstances. That day, the stately trees of Schwarzwalde became the background for massacre, the last sight that would be seen by those in the column I had run from. That column was marched into the forest and machine-gunned. One-quarter of Bissingen's inmates were killed. Only a few men lived to tell of this atrocity, one of them a distant cousin who survived by playing dead. Only Jack's stubbornness had, unwittingly, saved our lives.

The remaining three columns were counted, given rations for one day, and marched to the railway station. We were closely guarded by the S.S., which counted and recounted us as if we were some rare commodity.

Again, we were herded aboard cattle cars, sixty of us in each. We were near the end of our will to live. As we climbed on, Jack said to me, "Oh, God! Not these dirty, cold cattle wagons again."

"There is no other way. There is no other choice," I replied. It was ride or die.

"Are you willing to give up?" I asked.

We settled down on the floor of the car, which was attached to a boxcar loaded with bread, barrels of marmalade, and other food for the S.S. and for the prisoners if the train was in transit longer than anticipated. The food was guarded by four S.S. men.

The train moved out, only days it would turn out, before the French army reached that part of Germany. I later found out my cousin Albert, from Paris, fought through the war with de Gaulle in the Free French army and was among those liberators. Our ride was the same as the others we had been on in recent weeks, but more draining because we had fewer resources and were worn down more quickly by the cold, the stink of urine, and the presence of the dying and the dead.

K.Z. Allach Dachau

Dachau, the infamous concentration camp that had been the first of that kind in Germany, was to have been our destination. There was, however, too little space there and so we were rerouted to Allach, a subcamp of Dachau.

Germany was in disarray, but few members of the S.S. would see the impending defeat even at that late hour. The killing of human beings went on apace, with those unlucky victims perishing on the threshold of freedom. Some of them died without names, their bodies swallowed by shallow graves or fumes of fire or wild animals roaming the prairies and meadows.

Famine set in during those last weeks of the camps as the supply of food for the prisoners diminished. Hundreds died daily of starvation, which hurts your guts while you are not even able to cry.

The last days epitomized the total war the Nazis conducted against the Jews and the cruelty, the brutality, the beastliness of their racial theory. They crushed life. Hitler and his henchmen, until the last days of their control, went on with their plan to exterminate all Jews from the European continent.

It was an irony that the German Reich saw the Jewish people as a major enemy. We were soldiers fighting only for one cause: to survive the beast that stalked Europe.

On the third day of our one-day journey, our train was attacked by the Royal Air Force, which dropped bombs and strafed it with machine-gun fire. The train's guards ran for cover, leaving us and the food car unsupervised. We prisoners panicked. The press of our bodies broke the doors of our car and we jumped out, seeking frantically for some kind of shelter. In the confusion, a couple of us, including Jack and me, snuck into the food car, dipped into the marmalade, and ate as much as panic and our shrunken stomachs would allow. Jack and I also cut up four loaves of bread and hid the pieces in our pants, making deep pockets of the legs by binding the cuffs with shoelaces. About five minutes passed from the start of the attack, until we, too, finally sought cover away from the train. The planes continued to circle and dive for about fifteen minutes more. When the all-clear came, the remaining guards rounded us up and held a roll call so we could be counted and the dead totalled. We had quite a few casualties with our only consolation that a few of the guards were also dead. The train itself was among the lost, disabled five to six miles short of the station we were headed to, so we were formed into marching columns to continue the rest of the way to Allach.

As we walked, we disposed of our bread, fearing it would be found during Entlausung at the new camp and lead to punishment. We ate as much as we could, washing it down with water at little leaf-covered ponds at which we stopped along the way. At these stops, fights would break out as breadless prisoners attacked, seeking to steal a crust or a crumb. As we walked, I traded half of one loaf for a pair of shoes for Jack, since his were worn out. The rest of the bread I distributed among friends from Bendin.

We marched into the new camp half-dead from exhaustion. We found there would be no Entlausung, which knowledge was a disappointment, since it meant we could have saved some bread. But Jack and I had the consolation that our stomachs were full for the first time in a long time, and Jack had halfway decent shoes.

We were assigned bunks. The beds were stacked in threes, and the weakest prisoners were given the upper bunks. As the assignments were made, the fight for individual survival continued, with everyone pleading for a lower bunk. I ended up with a middle bunk and Jack with an upper.

By this time, our company consisted almost exclusively of living skeletons, men of just skin and bones. We found that there was a women's camp adjacent to ours, separated from us by barbed wire. We could see the women walking around, their nakedness wrapped only with blankets. Their heads were hairless, shaved because of lice. Their chests were flat, their bodies fleshless. It was impossible to believe these creatures were young and, until recently, goodlooking women.

We despaired for humanity, bewailing among ourselves the tragedies that surrounded us. Even if there was a day of reckoning for these crimes, the Germans could never be paid adequately for them. How could god Almighty see his children suffer so much agony and so much pain? The glow of burning corpses—stacked and doused in gasoline—could be seen for miles, and the smell of burnt flesh made us, the living, daily vomit our starvation rations.

There was no work for us. All we had to do was sit around and wait to die. Now attrition, in the form of starvation and exhaustion, took the major toll. The capos left were more lenient, as they, too, were waiting to die.

The war was lost for the Germans. It was now only a matter of days. But we also lost. Millions did not reach the day of liberation, dying without knowing what would happen to the Nazis, leaving this life with a curse on their lips for the "civilized world," which was too late to save them. Though I had forgotten how to weep, my heart still bled for my fellow inmates.

We knew the war's end was near. The Russians were at the gates of Berlin. The Americans were in Bavaria, about thirty miles from Allach. We carried hope for life even though we were immersed in death.

I told Jack, "If we ever leave this godforsaken camp, it will be as liberated men."

Sometimes fiction overlay reality. Though I knew it would come, I could never visualize the day of liberation. How would it come? And where? Who from my family had survived such a Gehenna? Yet, without knowing, I was only seven days away from being liberated by the U.S. 3rd Army. The mighty German army was in disarray, beset by chaos. We could feel in our bones the coming defeat of Germany. That was all that mattered, and that we should live to see it.

On April 23, we were assembled, given two days' rations at the gate, and marched to another cattle train. This time, our destination was the "Lake of Starnberg," where transportees were stood on the edge of the lake and machine-gunned. That was to be our end, but the plans for our transport went awry.

There were three hundred camps of prisoners in German-occupied territory, and many members of the fragmented Nazi hierarchy wanted to cover up their atrocities as much as possible in the last days of the war, hiding the bigotry, the brutality, the horrors of the concentration camps by silencing the tongues that might speak against them.

Piles of corpses, left like dirty wash, were what the Allied forces encountered as they fought to victory, as they liberated the famous, and the not-so-famous, death camps.

I wondered what our liberators were thinking as they discovered evidence of cruelty beyond imagination. Could they eat? Did they vomit? Did they take pictures with captured German leaders to brag about when they returned home?

The truth of Hitler's concentration-camp state was emerging for the whole world to ponder, as was the mystery of how this man could take power over a "civilized" nation like Germany.

An incredulous world would also read about a former chicken-farmer, Himmler, a fanatic racist and apostle of violence who shared Hitler's racial theories and generated the murder and evil committed in the name of Germany toward their goal of wiping out European Jewry. Himmler told his S.S. that his practical anti-Semitism was the same as *Entlausung*. Getting rid of lice was not a question of ideology, he said; it was a matter of cleanliness. No other period in history has seen such cruelty on such a scale.

In those last days of the war in Europe, as we were again being shipped away, the Red Army fought its way into the heart of Berlin, and about 200 German soldiers garrisoned in Munich, about seven miles from Allach, unsuccessfully tried to take over that city's vital areas so they could peacefully surrender and end the bloodshed.

There were 2,000 prisoners on that final death train, but our tormentors were unable to complete our last journey. The U.S. Army was nearby, and the roads were blocked. The area under German control shrank daily. Our train wandered aimlessly back and forth among the spur lines in the area. We watched quietly from our confinement, not knowing what to make of our erratic travel. We knew only that Starnberg was not getting closer.

After two days, the train stopped, and we were allowed to stretch our legs. We were encircled by the Allies. There was no place for the train to go.

We were near a railway crossing at the edge of a village named Staltach. Nearby was a farmhouse from which the S.S. decided to get water. I was chosen to go with three other prisoners, under supervision of one guard, to bring water for the guards.

At the farm, I looked around for a way to slip away and hide. I was not sure where I would go, but I knew the Allied armies were close and thought I could reach them. I had no chance to slip away, however, since my companions and the guard followed me closely. I went into the barn, where I found a store of carrot and potato peels prepared for the pigs. I filled my shirt with the scraps, since I knew they would provide an unusually delicious and nourishing meal for my comrades.

The guard looked the other way as we gathered our meal. While some of the guards remained as heartless as ever, most of them had become more lenient as they sensed the end of their power.

We started back to the train. As we walked, I noticed some wild snails in the tall, damp grass and picked up a dozen or more of them to add to the larder. When we reached the train,

I shared the vegetable peels with my companions. Jack had a fit when I offered to share the live snails with him. He and the others refused.

"How can you eat a living creature?" they asked.

I replied, "If the French can eat snails as a delicacy, I can eat them in an emergency."

And an emergency it was. We had eaten little for three days. If I had only had a little bit of salt, they would have tasted delicious. I bit the snails in half and swallowed them with my comrades looking on as if I were crazy. I can assure you that I got my vitamins for that day.

Staltach Junction

We sat where we were for two days without incident. Then, on April 27, a group of French-speaking Swiss from the International Red Cross appeared at our rail stop. They asked the guard commander, an S.S. Totdkopf captain, how many prisoners were on the train and where it was going. He refused to answer.

They asked the prisoners the same question. I, speaking in the broken French I had learned in Blechhammer working with French electricians, told them there were about 2,000 of us, mostly Jews, destined for disposal at Lake Starnberg.

The Red Cross men walked over to the commander and told him in no doubtful terms that he would be personally responsible for the safety and lives of all the prisoners on the transport and all of the guards would pay with their own lives if we were moved any farther. They said the American army was only ten miles away and they should arrive in a day or two. They added that 2,000 Red Cross packages would be delivered for distribution to us and they expected his full cooperation.

Since we could hear artillery nearby, the commander agreed to all these conditions.

That afternoon, two trucks loaded with the Red Cross packages arrived. The packages held chocolate, powdered milk, sardines, cocoa, cheese, and other things I can't recall. Our car received six extra packages, the contents of which became common property. Almost everybody opened his package at once and started eating all those goodies. A lot of them got very sick, including Jack, who gorged himself. When he saw all that long-denied food, his rationing instinct deserted him, and he couldn't stop eating. Something told me, however, that the end of our ordeal was near and I could relax. I ate only my chocolate.

During the next couple of days, I cared for my brother and helped, as I could, my other companions. We camped inside the cars and along the track. Jack was in pain, and I tried desperately to help him, though I was nearly helpless with the meager resources at hand.

On the second day after the Red Cross delivered its packages, I sat heating some water with powdered milk in a can over a little fire I had started. I had been using that warm milk to soothe Jack. The water was near boiling when one of the S.S. guards who still were overseeing us, came by and kicked the can over and away. I was furious. If my eyes could have killed, that arrogant S.O.B. would have died on the spot, but he still was armed and I was weak and exhausted.

By Monday, April 30, artillery fire and shelling from tanks were so intensive that we took cover underneath the rail cars. That afternoon, the shelling stopped. Within fifteen minutes after the blessed silence set in, tanks appeared, coming toward us. We couldn't make out whose they were at first, but when they came near us we could see soldiers on foot, behind them, pointing their guns at the Germans and yelling *"Haende hoch"* (Hands up). Finally, we grasped what was happening.

I walked over to the S.S. guard standing nearby with his hands up and kicked him with all my power. It was the one who had kicked over the can of boiling water. I kicked him several times but still had little power to hurt. He remained standing; I fell to the ground. A sergeant came out of the tank and asked me, in German, why I was so angry. I told him the story and he hit the guard with the butt of his rifle.

As destiny would have it, he told me he was a Jew from Brooklyn. His group was a reconnaissance unit of Patton's 3rd Army. He said we didn't have to be afraid anymore; our misery was over. The regular troops behind them would take care of us as soon as they arrived, which he thought would be in no more than an hour. We thanked them, kissed the tanks, and realized that we were, at last, free. We could breathe easier. Only those who have lost their liberty can really appreciate "freedom."

Indeed, on that day all the world was to find it could breathe easier because, as we were being liberated, Hitler, with his newly wedded wife, Eva Braun, committed suicide.

In the commotion of our liberation, the prisoners stormed the food car of the transport train like wild animals. I wanted no part of that, but I soon found I had my own cause for panic. In the process of kicking the S.S. guard, I had been separated from Jack. I couldn't find him anywhere. Finally, despairing, I walked to the nearby railroad crossing of the road into Staltach, went into the gatehouse the crossing guard used, sat down, and took inventory.

I couldn't believe that my hopes of liberation had become reality, that I had traveled so far, losing so many companions, and had survived to travel farther.

I felt as if a great weight had been lifted; as if I were floating. My thoughts returned constantly to one idea: "I'm free," in the center of a cloud composed of all the ramifications of that word—free!

I thanked Heaven for the grace granted me. I weighed only eighty pounds. I touched myself to see if it was really me. I fought to separate reality from illusion. Had it really happened at last? Was I really free again or was this another dream? I saw and felt through senses refreshed, rid of the bonds that had held my body and mind.

What was I to do next? Who had survived and who had perished in the holocaust? Where should I turn? Of only one thing was I sure: I did not want to go back to the place of my birth. There, I was not wanted. I had lived all those years of my growing up as a second-class citizen. I had wanted better then, and now there were no ties to prevent my seeking it. The order had changed, and the borders shifted.

There was relief in my heart, but at the same time a nagging pain. Nobody can cherish freedom more than we who had lost it, not for being criminals but just for being born into the Jewish faith. My mind was in a fog, my thoughts jumbled, my presence unreal. Free! I couldn't believe it.

I decided that the first step toward sorting out the chaos was to find shelter and to wash thoroughly. I had to clean up and find a place to sleep until things became more clear. Then I could resume life. I set out for the house next to the railway crossing. It was as good as any other place. I wasn't looking for luxury; anything was better than the railway car of my immediate past. I carried my only possession: the Red Cross package I had received two days before.

Spring was in the air. Life, so precious, fought for with so much courage and patience, took on the smell of flowers' blossoming. The birds' songs had an unfettered, lilting sound. All my surroundings came alive. I wanted to hug and kiss everybody coming my way—except the Germans. Their cruelty would take me a long time to forget and would never be forgiven.

My mind continued to whirl with a thousand and one thoughts as I approached the house. I knocked and politely asked the owner, in fluent German, if he would permit me to sleep over for a day or two and if he would help me clean up by permitting me to take a bath. His answer was a warm "Come on in." Four other men from our train were already guests in the house.

I went inside and headed directly toward the bathroom. A hot bath did wonders for my body. I bathed for much longer than a usual bath time, soaking in the warmth and freshness. I didn't want to leave the good feeling I had missed for such a long, long time.

When I finished bathing, I asked my host if it were possible to get clean underwear and a clean shirt. He replied positively and I felt so good, so alive, so like a newborn, that perhaps I was born anew. I washed all the suffering of the past five years into that one long, hot bath. The German hostess cooked a delicious dinner, which I politely refused, perhaps from instinct, perhaps from common sense, and perhaps because someone was watching over me. I asked only for hot water. I ate the cocoa from the Red Cross package for the next three days and nothing else. Thanks to this, I never got sick for a single day, unlike my companions, who took mounds of food into unprepared stomachs. My insides began to feel good again.

After dinner, we talked with our hosts. They had never been Nazis. They had not known about the camps. They were good Germans, and so were all the others we happened to talk to, and yet, every tenth German was a murderer of one Jew, and this had not been done in a vacuum. We were walking among them, living for the moment in their environment, and we couldn't recognize any of them as being murderers. They were so polite, so helpful, so God-fearing, and, at the same time, so false. Their only concern was the Allied occupational forces in their area, which provided incentive for most—but not all—of them to be polite to us.

Our host told me the summer house of the *Gauleiter* (governor) of all Bavaria was nearby, and that his cellar was filled with "goodies." I made it my goal to look up that bigshot the very next day.

When bedtime came, we were given the very comfortable beds of our hosts. This was very nice, but, after trying one, I had to refuse. I had a long way to go before I would be comfortable sleeping in a bed. I lay on the bare floor, falling into a long, sound sleep, secure in the knowledge that the Yankee army was all around me.

I prayed that they would be guarded in all their endeavors, asking God to protect them. My heart was full of eternal gratitude for the soldiers and for the humane American people. At last, right had prevailed over wrong, good over evil, light over darkness. Humanity had defeated the beast. I could once more dream of and plan for a better tomorrow, a better world with all humanity living in peace, without discrimination, without masters or slaves. My whole body was atremble. I was a free man again.

I awoke the next morning to a clear sky, with the air crisp

and dry. I could feel the season throughout my body. I washed, dressed, and had two glasses of very hot chocolate milk for breakfast. It warmed my body and made me feel good.

I set out to find my brother, walking through the whole village and asking all the survivors from our transport if they knew where Jack was. All answers were negative, but I knew he was alive and put my mind at ease. I didn't give up looking and asking, but I decided to pause and get rid of my striped suit. I had had enough of looking like a zebra. Even though nobody had papers and the war was still going on, I didn't feel I needed the stripes for identification. The tattooed number on my left forearm was a permanent identity card, which I would carry with me as long as I lived.

As I walked around the small village, I saw many other liberated men wandering around sick or half-sick and utterly helpless. We were waiting for the Allied forces, but these were taking their time to arrive. The promised one-hour waiting time had long since elapsed. The village was on a side road, and nobody would bother to occupy it until later in the week.

I set out for the *Gauleiter's* summer home, which was about 500 yards from where I was staying. I entered the two-story building, which contained two apartments, and was directed to the second floor. I knocked and the door opened. A middle-aged woman looked at me and started to cry, pleading with me not to harm her. I had no such thoughts in my mind. I asked for keys to the cellar. The woman and a younger companion were crying, and the older one fell to her knees at my feet. For a moment I visualized my mother falling before a German's knees, pleading for her life. I coaxed her back to her feet and finally convinced her that all I wanted was a suitable pair of pants and a jacket. They finally gave me the key. I walked down, opened the door, and looked in. I was flabbergasted. The cellar was stacked floor to ceiling with loot from all over Europe. I didn't know where to look first. God Almighty, what the Germans had stolen: furs from Belgium, perfume from Paris, soap from Russia, suits from Greece, nylons from Holland, silk underwear from Poland, shoes from Czechoslovakia. There were sacks of German paper money, which I thought was worthless. I found later that I was wrong.

It made me ill to think of how many people were deprived of their homes, property, and lives to provide such a stock for this pig. I just couldn't believe my eyes. I had to touch all those things to sense their reality. I tried on a suit. It fit, so I packed it in a small suitcase I picked up. Later, I would wear it to be married. I also packed six pairs of underwear, six pairs of socks, twelve handkerchiefs, a little manicure set, and two pairs of shoes. I dressed in pants, a shirt, and a jacket and walked out, leaving the door open. I wasn't about to return the key to the Gauleiter's wife. I threw it away.

I walked back to my temporary residence, where I urged my companions to go and change clothes. They did, and so did twenty other men and some women who had been liberated from another train, which had stalled near Staltach. Some of them loaded loot on hand wagons, stacking up everything from fine scents to fur coats and pulling them with their weakened bodies, headed for their pre-war homes.

I, for the first time in years, took a bath, shaved and dressed in normal clothes. I began to look like a human being again and felt stronger and healthier by the hour.

Some former prisoners needed medical help badly. They became sick the day they were liberated, eating pork and fats, which were, for some of them, like poison. The local Germans helped a lot, but it wasn't enough. For some, medical help came too late, but at least they died free men and were buried properly, though that would have been little consolation to them.

Jack was among those who became sick. When we were freed, he had eaten too much and then started to walk to the farm where we had been getting water. He had just wanted to get away from that train, which represented our years of suffering. He became ill as he walked, but managed to reach the farm, where he was nursed back to health. It was five weeks before I would find him again.

On the fourth day after liberation, the Allied Expeditionary Force arrived at Staltach in big military trucks. They moved the critically sick to hospitals, clinics and any other medical facility available. Those of us who were reasonably healthy were gathered and urged to go to a Displaced Persons camp at Landsberg, a former military camp on the River Lech.

Some of the freed men decided to go to their former homes. They started walking, often somewhat aimlessly and always without identification. Some made it to their goals, but some were killed by stray German soldiers who were still hiding around the countryside, unaware their war was lost and over.

I decided to trust the liberators and take one of the trucks to Landsberg am Lech.

Artilerie Kaserne Landsberg Lech

Landsberg, where Hitler had written the Nazi bible, *Mein Kampf,* had been used as a boot camp and to train artillery units. It had been built to hold 5,000 to 6,000 soldiers in its stone and brick block buildings.

My four comrades from the house in Staltach and I took one big room and made ourselves at home as well as we could. We soon learned we were on our own.

Food was supplied by the U.S. Army, but we had to find cooks to prepare it. After a couple of weeks, representatives of the United Nations Relief and Rehabilitation Organization (U.N.R.R.O.) arrived to administer the camp. By then, there were about 1,000 inmates there, with more on the way. They urged us to elect or appoint people so we could run our own affairs. In the meantime, we had to deal with sick people who weren't ill enough to be taken to a hospital.

The camp was guarded by U.S. military personnel. We resented that, and we let the commanding officer know our feelings. He listened sympathetically but said he could do little about it. He had his orders. We didn't know if the Americans were protecting us from the Germans or the Germans from us.

After VE-Day, when the war officially ended, our camp became like Grand Central Station. People came and went as transports were formed to move former prisoners of all backgrounds back to their native countries. More than 5,000 people were in Landsberg at its peak.

My friends and I became leaders of the camp, helping coordinate the movement of people in and out, arranging room assignments and food. I was one of the healthiest of the former prisoners so I felt I had to help as much as I could.

We Jews were still nameless and stateless, filled with hope but short on prospects. It wasn't until July that we received personal identification cards from the military government showing our residency at the Artilerie Kaserne Landsberg Lech, stating our date and place of birth and including our pictures. We envied the people departing for their respective homes and their countries of origin.

I maintained my resolve not to return to my native Poland, which was now completely dominated by the Soviets.

As time went on, the whole gruesome story of the murder of one-third of the prewar Jewish population of Europe unfolded. I made up my mind to fight for a Jewish homeland, a Jewish state. We were the people of the Bible and had our own state long before the modern states came into existence. Had we had our own state still, the Holocaust would never have happened.

I would stand in the DP camp and scream for justice. I blamed the whole free world for our predicament, accusing it of being deaf and blind to our continuing sufferings. Some of us had dreamed that after being liberated each and every one of us would be flown away to the "Promised Land," but it was the defeated Germans who were free again, and we, their victims, were still in camps under guard.

After many inquiries, I found Jack again, fully recovered from his sickness, about ten miles from Landsberg. I picked him up and brought him with me to the camp. We were happy to be together again. I worked in the camp administration as chief of the working committee and had my hands full helping newly arrived refugees. I was in charge of distributing the ablebodied to work as they were needed in camp. People began to arrive from Poland, and I got my first news of my youngest brother, Sam. He had also survived and had celebrated his sixteenth birthday at the time of his liberation in early March from the concentration camp Waldenburg. I sent a special emissary to bring him out of Poland. Jack and I waited as patiently as we could for his arrival so we could be reunited. All of our comrades considered us very lucky to have survived. It was a rarity, three brothers from one family.

Our reunion finally became reality. The scene was indescribable. I was in seventh heaven. My two brothers cried, but my reservoir of tears was still not replenished.

After we had reassured each other that we were not mirages, Sam pulled out a linen pouch he carried by his heart and removed from it a paper which he unfolded and handed to me. With Jack behind me, I read with great sadness. The words were written on the October day in 1944 on which our beloved father died in concentration camp Kletendorf of malnutrition and exhaustion. It gave the date of his death and said he was buried in the Jewish cemetery in Breslau. A cousin of ours had been second in charge at the camp and managed somehow to get permission for him to be buried reasonably properly rather than lost in a mass burial or burning of nameless bodies.

We stood in silence for several minutes, thinking our private thoughts about Papa and his untimely death. Then spontaneously, almost as if on cue, the three of us started reciting the mourners' prayer for the dead. We knew Papa was a righteous, pious, strictly religious man, and this was the highest service we could do for him. It is written that after the mourners' prayer, the soul of the deceased lifts itself higher into Heaven, but we knew our prayer at that moment lifted our beloved father's soul much higher.

We inquired as best we could about Mother's fate. We managed to find out that she had been among the last deportees from Bendin in 1943. She was shipped to Birkenau, where she was gassed. She was forty-four, a young tree cut down, an innocent life ended by untimely and unnecessary death, like so many others.

In 1975, I would visit Birkenau and stand at the ramp where she stood when she arrived on the cattle train. I would walk the path down where she took her last steps. I would reach the place where she was cremated and stand in silence for a long time, unable to speak, my dear wife, Ruth, at my side. I would recite for her the mourners's prayer for the dead. It would be there, for the first time since the depths of the Holocaust, that I would be able to shed tears—tears of sorrow, tears of anger, tears for all those who left their bodies on this godforsaken ground, ground soaked with so much Jewish blood, so much innocent blood.

Though the dead couldn't lift themselves up in 1945, the living started to surface. The DP camp grew, taking on all facets of self-government, including officials duly elected by democratic procedures in October, 1945. I was a candidate for the camp council. I was defeated but continued to be active in a variety of positions, and was primarily responsible for organizing camp maintenance, sorting out the craftsmen among the survivors and putting them to work. We formed our own police force to handle any internal problems which developed. Schools were opened, managed by ORT (Organization for Rehabilitative Training), which was supported mainly by American Jewry. Kindergartens and grade schools were started for new arrivals from Russia and Poland, families that had lived through the war in Russia. Gifted children were sent to Switzerland for special education and specialization in trades or professions.

A school of nursing was opened, and a hospital established, managed by famous doctors who had survived the Holocaust. Repair shops were created to serve the needs of the camp. A weekly newspaper began to appear, reporting news from all over the world of interest to Jews.

All kinds of sports events were held.

Political organizations formed, with the most active backing a Jewish state in the land of the Bible. The Survivors, unwanted in their former homes and weary of a life of tribulation and second class citizenry, waged a stubborn fight for the right to immigrate to Palestine.

Many of those in the camp, and especially the leaders of the central committee, which was established in Munich to coordinate DP camps in the American Zone in Bavaria, encouraged and organized illegal immigration to Palestine.

We learned the reaction of the free world to our plight. The U.S.A. would not relax its strict immigration quotas. Great Britain was pitiless in blocking immigration to Palestine. Australia was admitting only agricultural workers. There seemed to be no choice but to break the English blockade and immigrate, by any means, to Palestine, and to establish a homeland for all those Jews wanting to live in their own land, like any other people on earth, and not be persecuted anymore.

Various dignitaries from Israel and former soldiers from the Jewish Brigade, which had fought with the Allies, asked those of us who were in camps to stand up and be counted for Israel. We were the best weapon to appeal to the conscience of the free world. We re-emphasized how the defeated Germans had returned to normal lives while their victims' futures remained suspended in Displaced Persons camps until someone had mercy and granted them immigration visas. These came in trickles, and then only to those with relatives at their destinations.

The central committee sought to apply, with the help of the Jewish Agency for Palestine, a single policy of emigration for all the camps under its purview. It became the dominant belief that action—legal or otherwise—must be taken to defy the British Labour government and its foreign secretary.

Patience in the camps teetered on a thin edge. Many sat idly, not knowing what their futures would bring, but many of our people applied for illegal immigration. Among these would be Jack.

The illegals constituted a vanguard and a most powerful political force in establishing the independent state of Israel.

Despite the relative calm of Landsberg, the lessons and goal of Hitler were not lost. New arrivals from Poland told of pogroms aimed at Jews which were taking place in the newly established People's Republic of Poland. The Jews again had to run for their lives. This news confirmed for us that you could not change a leopard's spots.

When Sam was liberated by the Red Army, his first steps had been toward Bendin. He arrived there to find the janitor living in our apartment. The janitor reacted as if he'd seen a ghost, with a shocked "You're still alive!!" It was as if he didn't believe a Jew could—or should—still be alive. Sam left quickly, never to return and look at those people again.

Jack and Sam joined in my decision not to return to Poland. That land had become a graveyard. We could not face the prospect of resuming life there.

Life went on in Landsberg. Daily, individuals and families arrived. Families were reunited, brother with brother, sister with sister. Their joy was momentary as they took inventory of those missing and recounted who had died and where. They noted all those whose fates were unknown and instituted inquiries about them. Many of those questions remain unanswered to this day.

Out of the ashes of catastrophe, people began to build new lives. It was as if the branches of a felled tree were pushed into the ground and started to blossom. The survivors trickled into Landsberg from the death camps, from the forests, where they had fought as partisans, from the holes and false identities they had used to hide from the terror.

There were weddings, with the newlyweds obtaining one-room apartments from the newly created housing office of the camp, and births.

I was among the lucky ones who married. Ruth Katz had arrived in Landsberg on her way to Palestine from a field hospital in Saxony, where she had been working for the U.S. Army. She had been on Aryan papers during the war, living in Germany and working as a surgical nurse and, later, as a midwife. We married on December 22, 1945, and moved into an apartment with two bedrooms, a kitchen and a bath. It was larger than most, since Jack and Sam lived with us.

At the wedding were Jack and Sam, my Aunt Lola, and all the dignitaries of the camp. My best man was Dr. Gringhouse, the chairman of the camp. We were married by an orthodox rabbi from Hungary who had survived Auschwitz.

Sam attended a trade school to learn to be a plumber, and graduated with honors. Jack was in charge of a block, living quarters for about eighty people. Ruth worked in the hospital, helping the sick.

There were fine charity organizations which helped make our lives more pleasant, groups like the U.N.R.R.O., American Joint Distribution Committee, the Hebrew Aid Society, ORT, the Jewish Agency for Palestine, the Jewish Brigade (which fought the Nazis in Europe as part of the British Army), and other relief groups whose names I have forgotten. The U.S. armed forces also helped.

We, however, were tired of charity. We wanted to be useful citizens again and earn our daily bread with our hands and sweat. People in the camp began to open small shops, providing tailoring, shoemaking, dressmaking, and other services. There were butchers and barbers. Commerce sprang up but it was only to be temporary, we hoped. The nonprofit organization "BayrElsches Hilfswerk" gave Ruth the job of organizing a clinic where Jewish women could deliver their babies. With this job came a car and an apartment near the town of Augsburg. Thus, we kept very active until we left Germany in the spring of 1948.

For recreation, we had a few American entertainers perform for us, and there were concerts by famous musicians and the Red Army Choir. We continued to be visited by members of the Executive Committee of the Jewish Agency, among them David Ben Gurion, I. Greenbaum, and other leaders from Palestine. We were all thrilled to hear about that land and their talks gave us hope for the future. These were the first times we could get firsthand regards from our brethren there.

Jack left Germany in the spring of 1946. When the time came for his departure, we tried to smile, but deep in our hearts we were sad to part again. This time, at least, the parting was voluntary, and we hoped to be reunited again, soon.

The immigrants were smuggled by an underground route. Jack was on a ship that was intercepted near the coast of Haifa and turned back to Cyprus, which was under British rule.

There, its illegal passengers were interned behind barbed wire again, to await their turns for permission to go as part of a legal quota from that island to Palestine.

Why do bad things happen to good people? All we were asking for was to be productive and live as a nation among other nations. All we asked for was the tiny piece of real estate that God promised to our forefathers, Abraham, Isaac, and Jacob.

In 1938, the Evian Conference had been convened under an initiative of President Franklin Roosevelt. Its purpose was to help emigration from Germany. Thirty-two nations sought to find a solution to that problem, but it soon became clear that all were reluctant to take any significant steps toward a solution. There were lengthy speeches, and a committee was set up in London that lacked funds and could not function. The conference accomplished nothing.

In 1943, another conference was convened, this time in Bermuda, to consider the problem of refugees. This conference, like the previous one, proposed no practical solution.

In 1946, the newly formed United Nations appointed a committee to study the British mandate on Palestine and the emigration of the displaced persons in the camps.

A massive protest took place in our camp when the U.N. commission arrived to take firsthand testimony from survivors of the Holocaust. The protest was mainly against the British government and its emigration policies, with some ire aimed at the U.S. Congress, which was slow to allow DPs to settle in the United States.

In November, 1946, I became the father of eight pounds of healthy baby boy. David was born at the Franciscan Hospital in Munich, the same town in which Naziism was born.

I debated with myself and with Ruth about foregoing circumcision since that had been an instant sign to the Nazis of who was Jewish. Ruth insisted on the religious ritual, stating that we were as good as any other people and we should not retreat from our belief. The others should feel their shame and guilt as long as they lived; we should not let them forget. "We are a proud people, with a stormy past, and whoever tried to destroy us, in the end, perished themselves," she said. I agreed on all counts.

The ritual, on the eighth day after the birth, was conducted by a Jewish *Moel*—religious surgeon—and attended by almost all the nuns and priests at the hospital, who had never before witnessed such a celebration. They even supplied special food and drinks for the occasion.

Acquiring a buggy for the baby was a special challenge. Nothing was available in the stores. I had to seek one from private citizens, and there was no way to advertise, so I stood in front of the hospital and asked each passerby if he had a buggy to sell. I must have talked with 10,000 people. It took about five days before I got results: a most beautiful blue-and-white buggy, the colors of the Jewish flag for my firstborn son. I was a happy father and relieved to be launching a new generation toward a new future and a better life than we had had so far.

By the end of 1946, Jack's papers were cleared for entry into Palestine from Cyprus. He worked hard there, trying to prepare a suitable home for us. He joined the Hagana, the underground "Jewish Defense Force" then active in British mandated Palestine. His assignments kept him busy evenings and, sometimes, nights. We now received mail at regular intervals and were pleased with Jack's accomplishments. Eventually, he would become a staff sergeant in the Israeli army.

People came through Landsberg looking for their families. Many left disappointed, not finding their loved ones. Sometimes, however, families were reunited, and the joy spread to everybody who witnessed their happiness.

In 1947, the United Nations voted to partition Palestine into a Jewish state and an Arab state. The Arabs rejected the resolution out of hand and promised the Jewish inhabitants of Palestine a bloodbath.

Illegal immigration was stepped up. People were needed to protect the promised state. Friends left weekly, their departures in strict confidence, without any unusual goodbyes, especially when they were males of military age and/or with military experience.

That year was also marked by the experience that inspired the book *Exodus,* when a ship was returned to Hamburg, Germany, by the British fleet.

In spring, 1948, we were told to be ready for transport. Ruth and I, and fifteen-month-old David, left in a convoy of military trucks. We carried only two suitcases, containing bare necessities. We traveled day and night.

Sam stayed in Landsberg, finishing his training as a plumber. He immigrated to the United States in 1949 with the help of the Hebrew Immigration Aid Society. He settled in Kansas City, Missouri, but he couldn't get a union card as a plumber. Temporarily, he thought, he worked in a watch repair shop, where he got promoted to traveling salesman. Eventually, he formed his own company and became a successful businessman.

Another milestone in my life, passed with a sigh of relief, came when we reached Saarbrucken and crossed the border into France. We had left Germany; we were out of the lion's den.

We crossed France, toward the Mediterranean Sea, stopping at a transit camp near Marseilles for temporary shelter. The camp, supported by the French government, was used by all illegal immigrants to Palestine.

After we were in that camp for about a week, we were told to get ready. That night was our "D" (for departure) day. We had to be ready after midnight. Our transport consisted of 2,000 young men and women and about three families with children to provide a cover and/or buffer in case we were stopped by the British navy. Quietly, we boarded our ship, a former presidential yacht, which normally held no more than 200 people. At first sight, the boat reminded me of Buchenwald. The hold contained a three-level stack of boxes, with each box holding four people. As a family, we got a larger box. The sanitary conditions fell short of being suitable for humans. There were portable toilets and showers on deck. During the day, most of us had to stay below deck in stifling, stuffy surroundings. With the exception of the families with small children, the passengers were only allowed on deck at night.

The crossing was slow and tedious. A trip that normally took four or five days dragged into fourteen. We were heavily loaded, and this made the trip longer. We were also stalling somewhat because the declaration of Israel's independence was pending. In fact, by the time we came within sight of the breathtaking scenery of our promised land, we were legal. Israel had declared its rebirth as a nation. As we pulled into the harbor of Haifa, we were greeted by our countrymen from all walks of life. We joined in the celebration of our newly proclaimed and established state of Israel, and in the battle to assure that freedom, waging war against five invading neighboring Arab countries.

The young men from our ship were taken straight from the ship to the front lines, some without even tasting a loaf of bread. Many died for our country, but at least they died with weapons in their hands, knowing their lives were not wasted. They died for a better tomorrow for the Jewish people, and for all mankind. They died so their people could be free.

My travels were over. I was fully free at last.

Reunited with Jack in Landsberg/Lech, Bavaria (1945)

Sam, Jack, and Harry, reunited at Sam's wedding (1957)

Uncle Samuel (standing) in the Polish army.
All his family perished in Auschwitz.

Our wedding (December, 1945)

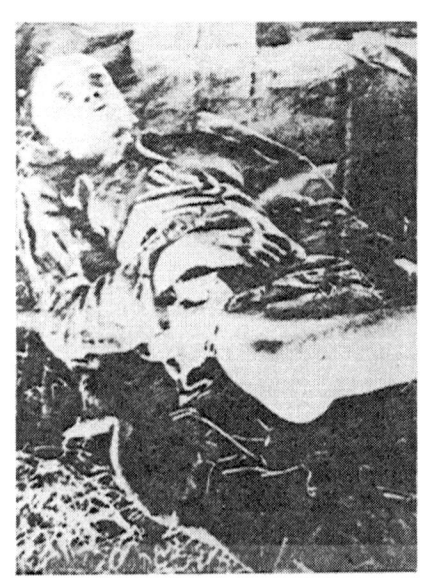

Öfen, in denen die Leichen verbrannt wurden.

:he Einwohner von Gardelegen müssen die Gräber für die Ermordeten

sinnen aus den stickigen Baracken heraus auf freie Gelände, wo die Leichenhaufen in den ersten Tagen immer noch anwuchsen.

Epilogue

Our people fought for the survival of a nation that was born after the destruction of one-third of us in Europe. These dead had gone to their deaths not knowing that they shared in the genesis of a new nation, giving incentive to us, the living, to carry on in our just cause. Every life in Israel was precious; everyone killed in the war of independence was part of a close-knit family.

A famous Jewish fighter of the 1920s once said: "It is good to die for one's country."

So, again, we buried the dead. The struggle for survival in dignity of an ancient people went on and on and on, and how it would end, nobody knew. To this day, no one knows. The time is overdue for the Jewish people to find peace and a life among the nations of the world.

Israel has had outstanding success in the years of its existence, transforming the desert into a rich, abundant and beautiful country. It is a monument to the human spirit, a nation where uncompromising fortitude and human ingenuity have withstood and conquered both natural and manmade obstacles.

Israel's achievements provide people all over the world with a sense of pride. Its learning institutions have standards among the highest anywhere. Its contributions to all fields of science, technology, agriculture, and art are numerous.

The Israelis know what they have achieved and are proud of it. They have stood up and asserted their rights in the face of scolding, negative world opinion. They have thoroughly stated their principles. They have taken in over a million refugees from all over the globe—the tired, the sick, the poor, the persecuted, the rejected—and made them proud and useful citizens, a joy to this generation and all generations to follow.

May God protect Israel and its people, and all mankind. Amen!!

Of more then 300 members of our family in prewar times, about thirty survived:

My brother Jack married our French cousin Sabine, herself a survivor of Auschwitz. He lives in Paris, where he is a successful businessman. He has two married children.

My brother Sam still lives in Kansas City, where he lives with his lovely wife, Ann, and daughter Gisselle.

My cousin Serge survived. He is retired and lives with his family in France.

My friend Israel was hanged in 1943, trying to escape with two other inmates.

Sarah Kukulka, Israel's girlfriend, was a leader of the uprising of the Bendin Ghetto and died with a gun in her hand.

Baruch Gaftek, my first Colony Elder in Mangersdorf, escaped from camp. He was also a leader of the Ghetto uprising, fighting the Nazis to the last.

Judith Firstenfield was deported to Berkenau in 1943, on the same transport as our mother. They were gassed.

Mary Kokocinska survived and went to Sweden after the war.

DEC. 1982

To my dear Saba,

This book gave me pleasure to all extent. It touched me that you re-lived your "war years" for me. I think my question when I was 3 has been answered.

I now know the pain & suffering you & others went through. This is something I had not known.

I don't agree at all with Beth about needing history. My father says the same (as Beth) This book isn't a history book it's a factual story of your life. It should be yours to write in any way. It was what happened to YOU!

I'd rate your book a 13 on a 1 to 10 scale. It was fabulous Remember, I love you And let God Bless you as he has.

Love,
Ari

Why didn't they bomb Auschwitz?

Reflections of a survivor

By HARRY POSMANTIER

A Sentinel exclusive

It is now 50 years since the defeat of the Nazi beast, which threw humanity into the dark ages.
We Survivors now celebrate! Fifty years ago we were liberated from the Nazi Death Camps.
For 50 years I have lived and relived the horror of that Nazi past.
Even until today, I avoid driving by factories with big chimneys, which remind me of the smoke and smell of burned flesh from the ovens in the camps; Chimneys which bring back the image of my mother engulfed in flames; the image of bars of soap made from the rendered bodies of the millions less fortunate than I and imprinted with the letters "RIF" – Rein Judisch Fett. Pure Jewish Fat.
Even until today, I avoid traveling by train, which reminds me of the crowded cattle wagons in which I and thousands of others were jammed so we could do nothing but stand as we were shipped from Gross Rosen to Buchenwald, from Buchenwald to Bissengen, from Bissengen to Allach-Dachau, from Dachau to Starnberg Lake – our final destination where we were to be

disposed of, following in the trajectory of thousands who had been stood on the lake's edge and machine gunned. The click, clack of rails registers an alarm in my whole body, and I still tremble.

Even until today, I wake up in a sweat, chased by Nazi guns, surrounded by SS men with dogs at their sides. I wake up screaming in the dark night, afraid for the well being of my children and grandchildren, who lie safely asleep in their own beds, never – as long as we remember – to be awakened from a nightmare to find it has become a reality.

My name is Harry Posmantier. I was 19 in October, 1940, when I was taken by Germans from my home in Poland to Germany proper. It was the beginning of a horrible odyssey that began in the Highway Camp of Klein Mangerdorf III and ran its tortured 54 month course through a dozen forced labor camps and concentration camps, ending at a railroad junction in the Bavarian woods. We lived constantly with the stench of death. Along the way – at Blechhammer, a subcamp of Auschwitz – I acquired the tattooed number – 178246 – which I carry on my left forearm even until today.

Two thousands of us were liberated by the American Third Army on that railroad junction near Munich. It was April 30, 1945, the day Hitler commited suicide, I was 24.

After liberation, the Americans moved us to various military camps. In a camp for displaced persons at Landsberg am Lech I met and married Ruth Katz, Today we reside in Skokie, Illinois. We have two married children and five grandchildren, may God protect them and keep them forever.

When my eldest grandson, Eric, was three, he asked me: "Grandpa. Why do you have a number on your arm?" I told him I would explain when he got older. I wrote a book, "The Last of the Numbered Men," which was published in 1984 so he would know why, and remember.

Remembering, that is our obligation.

For we who survive, memory is the key to the future; to making sure the terrible events of the Holocaust will never be forgotten and never repeated.

The children who survived the Nazi camps are now well into middle age. Most of the adults who remain are elderly. Our ranks diminish. In a decade or two, there will be no more left of the numbered men and women.

We survived to bear witness; to demand justice wherever injustice or discrimination occur.

We survived to remember and to make sure that our memories do not die with us; to prepare the future generations for a time when there will no longer be living witnesses to those events – living witnesses to counter the lies of the apologists and revisionists and say: "The Holocaust did indeed happen! And as bad as the stories may seem, the reality was worse."

We are the conscience of the world; a reminder of the injustices that occurred and are occurring and can still occur wherever humanity closes its eyes and ears.

We are accusers, charging the world with being blind and deaf to the suffering of our people before and during World War II.

In a way, the world's disbelief can explained. That's why we must remember. Who could visualize that a people with the highest standard of education in all Europe – a nation most cultured and sophisticated – could follow a leader who was a monster in human flesh? Who could imagine a whole nation could be silent to all of those atrocities, which occurred in the name and with the silent approval of the German people?

We bear witness: education and sophistication are not guards against depravity.

Night fell on mankind 56 years ago when the Nazis decided to conquer and enslave peace-loving nations and to dominate all the world with their racist theories that relegated Jews and many others to the ranks of sub-humans. Among their goals was total annihilation of the Jewish people. Six million of our people -

a third of them innocent children – and many millions of non-Jews were killed.

This tragedy could have been averted had the French and English not appeased the "Fuhrer;" had the Soviets made a pact with England and the West instead of becoming allies with Hitler's traitorous Third Reich; had the Catholic Church and the Pope spoken out.

REFLECTIONS

We remember the killers and their helpers: Lithuanians, Poles and Ukrainians who worked with the Nazis to kill or dispose of the Jews.

We remember the collaborators: Austrians and Romanians who fought at the side of the Nazis; the Hungarians who helped liquidate their Jews; the French police who fervently sought out Jewish children to deliver to their Gestapo masters, and the Italian fascists who handed over their Jews to Germany's death camps.

We remember also that the allies knew what was going on in Auschwitz and other camps and didn't do enough to stop it in time to save Jewish lives. We know that whenever factories started synthesizing gasoline, the Allies bombed them immediately and with precision. The camps of Auschwitz were only miles away, and other camps were near other factories. Would some prisoners have died? Probably. But thousands of victims would have been saved.

We bear witness: the killing did not end with the end of the War.

We remember the Survivors who returned to their homes in Poland and elsewhere after the Holocaust only to encounter neighbors still poisoned with hatred who launched pogroms which left their tortured fellow citizens dead or injured for life in their own villages.

Had we had a state of our own, this tragedy couldn't have happened. We had dreams for a better world, for a better tomorrow, for a better future for our children. Instead, we feared for their lives.

We Jews suffered from the cross, double cross and twisted cross, burned as non-believers and Christ killers. Jews have been – and are being - killed in the Olympic village of Munich; in synagogues and restaurants in Paris and in Ankara, in Buenos Aries and in London.

We are not secure even in the houses of worship where we pray, cry, complain of our misfortune and ask forgiveness for our sins. There is no answer to our plea. Are we to be victims forever? Are we to be killed so senselessly as the world looks on and says "Amen. They are only Jews."

Was not Auschwitz enough? Can the world survive another Auschwitz? Can the world be indifferent to the goings on?

We remember that it is just not Jews who are still being killed in the name of religion, ethnicity and tribalism. It is not only Jews who are targets of genocide, as we witness in Eastern Europe and Central Africa. Catholics kill Protestants and vice versa. Islamic fundamentalists kill moderate Muslims who don't agree with their policies.

We must remember the signals from the past, and we must act if we are to survive.

We also remember the good, lest we be buried in terror without hope.

We remember our heroes who fought the Nazis in the ghettos, and in the forests of Central Europe as partisans.

We remember the thousands of Jewish soldiers who died fighting on the Allied side during World war II until victory was achieved.

We remember those who fought and died for a free Jewish state of Israel.

And we remember the righteous gentiles. The Danes and others who hid Jewish children, risking their lives and those of their families. We remember the soldiers of all backgrounds who fought the Nazi horror and helped us Survivors find our ways back to life.

Blessed be their memory forever.

We remember, and we plead. We ask, again, all free people to take a stand against the terrorists of the world whose hideous crimes, committed daily, disrupt the lives of all of us as they maim and kill indiscriminately. It is time to take a stand against all who preach hatred; to unite and fight that this tragedy should not be repeated because the world cannot survive another Holocaust.

Those of us who survived are obligated to remain alert; to remember this darkest of tragedies – but with hope:

Hope that the memories will strengthen mankind's struggle for peace.

Hope for human dignity rather than deprivation; for building, not destroying; for love, not hate.

Hope for a better tomorrow for all men and women and children, with people brought together and taught to do away with slaves and masters.

There is no master race, only the human race. There is no blue blood, only the red blood of people created equal.

It is in the memory that we learn the price of hate. Either we will live together or perish together, and my prayer is for life.

My eternal gratitude to the American people and the American 3rd Army – my liberators.

1995 A.D.